MY BROTHER'S KEEPER

ABOVE & BEYOND "THE DOTTED LINE"
WITH THE NFL'S MOST ETHICAL AGENT

BY

EUGENE LEE

FOREWORD BY OMARI HARDWICK

Cover photo of Eugene Lee by Barry Lee Moe

ISBN: 978-1-944109-00-4 (print)
ISBN: 978-1-944109-01-1 (ebook)

Published by Vesuvian Books
www.vesuvianbooks.com

Printed and bound in the United States of America

Contents

Dedication

....

This book is written for my late father, Peter W. Lee, who dreamed the dream with me and set the standard of honor and humility to which I aspire each and every day, for my mother whose courage, caring heart and unconditional love continue to strengthen and inspire, and for my loving wife Leslie without whose selfless sacrifice, unwavering support and boundless love, this book would not have been possible. For Lucas and Vivienne.

Foreword

··

by Omari Hardwick

How interesting in this journey of life are the pebbles we kick inadvertently while just trying to keep our pace on the yellow cracked road. Sometimes this pebble comes in the form of a tree subtly sitting beside a dusty peaceful path in which either letters, words or names we deem significant are carved on the bark. Sometimes it's a place that seems to come out of nowhere while enroute to a designated destination. Over time, we discover that this unexpected locale becomes one of more significance to where we are going in the future than that of familiarity. Moreover, sometimes this pebble comes in the form of another human being who appears in the mundanity of your run of the mill, solid enough gymnasium located at the lobby level of a Brooklyn New York apartment building.

The year was 2013, in the autumn of a city signified by its "never sleep" moniker, and I was in my never sleep norm attempting to give some love to my "aging" 39 year old ex-athlete frame. I had recently relocated from the city of Lost Angels with my family to the city that once served as the genesis to my journey as a professional artist. We were in New York—or shall we say Old York, given my long-standing history and love of the Big Apple—to start a job I'd recently booked that would film in the city as well as the boroughs of BrookLINE, Bronx, and Queens. I had just completed a lower body workout, and in my haste to get back upstairs and dive into more studying, I had mistakenly, and atypically, left out the equipment I'd used. The following day, there was a reprimand from quite a stout pebble who looked to be no stranger to the gym. For the athlete, the artist, the man's man, and son to an active father by nature and nurture, I embraced readily this scolding for leaving out the weights that the women of the complex would not be able to put back—as stated by the gentleman who approached. I will never contend to know everything. However, I confidently know what I know, and what I do know is life is much more manageable for those of us who desire to be checked for our indiscretions—our oopsies even. This pebble in essence had done the kicking. Its name, Eugene Lee, and its size, about that of mine when I played ball.

"Hey man, I'm Eugene. I saw you left the weights on the bar yesterday. You know we have women who have a harder time getting these heavy weights off, man. You gotta re-rack your weights after your workout!"

My reply with fervor, "Absolutely! You got it Eugene … I wasn't thinking. My bad! I'm Omari. Nice to meet you."

The weeks to follow, we started to see each other every time we would work out and eventually asked what life had each other doing. Eugene told me he was an attorney and more specifically, an NFL agent. I expressed the irony in my having worked out for the NFL and having a free agent shot. I further spoke of the fact that my father was not only an attorney; but at one point tried his hand at sports agenting for the NFL, before deciding there was too much corruption and arrogance, namely from the players. Eugene and I immediately discovered we knew some of the same characters associated with the world putting food on Eugene's table. I shared with him that now I was an actor and a recent job had moved my family and me to the city. He spoke of his wife, Leslie, being someone pursuing a career in acting and as men innately do so much better than our fairer gender, we verbally put out in the cosmos that we should chop up life more over a beer sometime, when both our insanely packed schedules allowed. This gym had ultimately provided me with my first friend in the building.

The journey ahead would reveal how much we viewed life alike—from our poetic ways of looking at it, to similar feelings about our fathers, our respect for our mothers and women in general, the pain in death we had both endured, our love of laughter, our tenacious attack professionally, and the passion with which we loved ... rivaling of course our temper of equal passion. Eugene T. Lee (with perhaps God allowing the T to stand for this tenacity I speak of), son of Lucy and Peter Lee, and brother to David, would eventually have that "beer" coming more in the form of whiskey as we both quickly learned we had even more in common in our kinship with such a beverage. Perhaps we are both old souls. Most who know me would say this is an understatement; while undeniable for Eugene as well, it was refreshing for me that, when we met, he possessed enough of the young soul I always had but was trying to regain, and would become the person in many regards to bring this back into my life and soul. He enjoyed the laughter of life so much it became hard to know when he was being serious. But upon learning his memory was as photographic as mine (only gifted by God to those who have a unique job on this planet), that he had very colorful, soulful, and strong political and cultural perspectives, which made me feel at home, and that he had a desire to grow his family ... I knew he was a great and rare combination man of range. These were the types of men I had always gravitated toward even as a young boy, let alone as a grown "boy."

My new pebble of a friend I had nicknamed, "Eugo," not only for his huge shoulders and arms, but also for his huge blueprints for his life. One of these hefty blueprints involved his merging my life of acting with his of agenting. He often represented young men as brown as he and I who were hopeful like thousands before ... that playing football on Sunday was a "Robin Hood" way to take from billionaire team owners to feed the poor while bring smiles not only to themselves, but to the proverbial family who would surely be in tow. Eugo would set out as President and CEO of his own sports agenting group, and be featured in a documentary, 'The Dotted Line,' about the maintenance of the ethical approach to protecting these young warriors and securing their dreams and future.

Eugene Lee would soon set his sights on penning his first book. I say first because I cannot fathom the man I am proud to know and call friend, stopping at one book. Eugo has too much to say, and I honestly think he is not only called to change the face of sports agenting, but I believe his call is to these young men and making them better. That is the most important trait of mutuality we share. Our love for youth and aiding their journey where otherwise the pebbles could prove to be shards of glass and rusted nails. I love Eugene for this kind of dedication to humanity, to our young men who we both feel compelled to help to be what God intended; leaders of the next generation.

Speaking of the next generation, somewhere within the

threads of the following pages you will cloak yourselves in, lies a journal, a message, a poem to be revered by Eugene and Leslie Lee's future children. A memoir of sorts revealing even more of this man who will rock his children to sleep singing ABCs, as he has as uncle to mine.

As Dickens once wrote in *A Tale of Two Cities*, "It was the best of times, it was the worst of times, it was the age of wisdom, it was the age of foolishness, it was the epoch of incredulity, it was the season of Darkness, it was the spring of hope, it was the winter of despair." He went further to say, "The period was so far like the present, that some of its noisiest authorities insisted on its being received, for good or for evil, in the superlative degree of comparison only." If only this legendary scribe knew just how prophetic he was. We are still in the best of times and the worst of times. With technological advances and scientific discoveries, we are entering a Golden Age of health and prosperity in this country. However, we still have the paralyzing pestilence of race relations, political scandals and extreme poverty afflicting this great nation.

The pride I ultimately have in this effort by my friend, my Eugo, is that he has bravely chosen to make himself one of these noisy authorities of this era, holding his conch and screaming his belief that beauty can exist in the battle called life; and even in the sport serving as a microcosm of life, involving monsters called players who don't get enough credit for their ability to run the real monsters of life away. Eugene Lee has chosen to run down his field with the same passion and urgency as the players he represents run down theirs. And, he, like most sound and special men, has shared many an equally special quote with me. The greatest however is the simple one I could hear over and over again; "Real recognizes real." Well, Eugo, you are correct, and what I recognize is that Papa Pete is REALLY proud of his boy. And, again, so is the pebble you tossed in your pocket for disregarding the rules.

Introduction

······························

I Am My Brother's Keeper

I am my brother's keeper. Helping others realize their dreams all the while steering them around a litany of obstacles, shielding them from a host of problems, protecting them from an army of detractors—in some cases themselves—is not just my job, it's my calling.

In South Bend, Indiana, football is king. I'm here on a weekend trip for the Notre Dame Spring Game, to meet with Irish standouts Justin Tuck and Ryan Grant. These are two elite, blue-chip prospects, with high profiles and even higher expectations.

Tuck has been nicknamed "The Freak" by his teammates, because of his exceptional size (6'5" 270) and athletic ability. He will eventually break Notre Dame's all-time record for sacks. Grant has prototypical NFL running back size at 6'0 and 225lbs, and has earned accolades around the football office for his exceptional attitude and patience. He has worked hard and quietly waited his turn as other highly touted Irish backs have come and gone.

Looking around one of college football's most historic stadiums, which is almost full in spite of the fact fans are on hand to watch a scrimmage, I'm reminded of what's at stake. There are thousands of grown men walking around in Notre Dame jerseys—those worn on the field by young men who are barely twenty. Somewhere in the stands are parents who raised and cared for these athletes and who watch every pile closely to make sure they get up. I'll meet with the players and their families, as many agents will before it is all said and done. As competitive as their business is, so is mine. When I turn in my rental car and board my flight back to New York, I will do so, hopefully, with a sense of encouragement after these meetings, with two men whom I know to possess high character. Part of the nature of the business is I will have spent money on something—signing these players—that is in no way a sure thing. You have to look for encouragement wherever you can find it in this business. Sometimes it's a hug from a parent on the way out of the stadium. Sometimes it's a reassuring text from a player. Other times it's just knowing you gave a great presentation.

My journey to signing Tuck or Grant will include many more rental car miles, plane tickets, texts, emails and phone calls. Then the real challenge begins the NFL.

If they succeed, I succeed. If they fail, I fail. It is symbiosis in the truest sense of the word. Of course; the road is far from smooth. There are potholes deeper than chasms and bumps taller than mountains. Nevertheless, if the road was perfectly paved everyone would travel it, and my services and expertise would be unnecessary. Leave it to a sports agent to employ a travel analogy. We do a lot of it. We watch many games, recruit a lot of young men, and experience the joys and sorrows of the players we represent.

It's the ecstasy of a signed contract and the agony of a torn Achilles. And I couldn't imagine doing anything else.

It's why I left the financial guarantee and long-term security of a position with a well-respected New York law firm and opted to risk everything on one endeavor with ETL Associates, Inc. However, unlike many other sports agencies that cater to professional athletes in a smorgasbord of sports, I ditched the opportunity to be a jack-of-all-trades, master-of-none and focused all my energies on the National Football League and the athletes looking to make pro football their livelihood.

However, that's not the only difference.

I vet my potential clients just as much as they vet me. I don't just seek out the athletes with the fastest 40-yard dash times, the most bench press reps, or the highest vertical leaps—I want the guys with the best moral fiber and character. Players who will make just as big an impact in their communities as they will on the field. The kind of young men fathers want their sons to emulate and mothers want their daughters to marry.

When an NFL team interviews, tries out or ultimately signs one of my players, they know without question they're dealing with an athlete who is a pro in every sense of the word; a player who is committed to giving his team and the city he's playing for everything he's got and more, whether he's in uniform or not.

Moreover, just as my players' commitment to their teams and teammates is unwavering, so, too, is my commitment to them, lasting well beyond their playing days. Not only do I strive to place them in the best possible situations for on-the-field success, but I will also do everything in my power to prepare them for the eventuality of that final snap and all that follows. We will forever be family. Brothers. And I will never desert my brother.

For the vast majority of aspiring pro football players it all starts with the NFL draft, the ultimate "pick me for your team" scenario. But unlike those elementary school gym class kickball games where getting picked last came with a certain amount of shame and embarrassment, just getting to the point of being NFL draft-eligible is a victory in itself.

First, consider the fact that only about 4% of the nation's high school football players actually have what it takes to play college ball. Bear in mind, I'm not just talking about the cream of the crop Division I football—I'm talking about college football of any type. But let's say you defied the odds, impressed the scouts, passed all your classes, got your HS diploma and put yourself in position to ball at the next level— the *highest* next level. At last count 128 American colleges and universities had NCAA Division I Football Bowl Subdivision programs (FBS), each with approximately 110 players per squad. Once again, let's say for argument's sake you've amassed considerable playing time during your collegiate career and are ready (or think you are) to make that giant leap into the pro game.

Since each Division I team averages 15 seniors, that's a total of 1,920 players coming out every year. Then there's Division I Football Championship Subdivision (FCS) (125 schools), Division II (168 schools), Division III (237 schools) and NAIA (73 schools) to consider. Sticking with the formula of 15 draft-eligible seniors per school adds another 9,045 players to the mix, bringing the total to 10,965 hopeful NFL'ers. Each year, there are a number of underclassmen who, having performed well enough to earn some (or perhaps considerable) attention and accolades, and lured by the fame and fortune of playing ball at the next level, opt to forego any further collegiate action and take their shot in the draft. It averages out to 65 players per year based upon the figures from the last few years. That brings the grand total to 11,030 players vying for selection by 1 of 32 NFL teams. But with a mere 254 draft picks in all, harsh reality dictates only 2.3% of that massive player pool will actually hear their names called.

Of course, being picked doesn't mean you're home free. Unless you're selected in one of the early rounds, thereby guaranteeing yourself a hefty signing bonus and, in all but the rarest cases, a spot on the final 53-man roster, you still have to do everything within your power (and then some) to make the team, or at the very least the 8-man practice squad.

Those who don't make it into an NFL training camp through the draft can still get there via free agency and, hopefully, impress the coaching staff enough to the point where they see you as something more than just another body to round out an offensive or defensive drill. Nevertheless, again, the road ahead of them is long and the climb is steep.

Big picture, when you lay it all out, and factor in the trades, injuries, salary caps, team needs, coaching changes, inside favors, outside influences, and a few dozen additional elements that are virtually impossible to fully comprehend, dreaming of becoming a professional football player and actually realizing that this dream is nearly impossible.

However, it does happen.

Tyreo Harrison typifies the model ETL Associates client. In 2001, his senior season, he led the team in tackles and earned honorable mention All-American honors from College Football News. But even more impressive, he was given the Nick Pietrosante Award, an annual, teammate-voted award given to the Irish player who best exemplifies courage, dedication, loyalty, pride and teamwork.

Tyreo represented everything that was right about college

football and college football players and I just had to be his agent. But like all college players who have proven themselves at that level and show potential to succeed at the next one, Tyreo had numerous suitors, most far more experienced and established than I was at the time.

Tyreo must have sensed that, recognized that we were cut from the same cloth, because he ultimately signed with me, although I'm sure it didn't hurt that we both went to school at ND.

The next step in Tyreo's pro football dream was the NFL Scouting Combine.

Now for those of you who are unfamiliar with that term, the NFL Combine is without question the greatest showcase for hopeful professional athletes in the world; a weeklong event where invited college football players are subjected to a vast array of physical and mental tests in front of an audience of NFL scouts, coaches and GMs. It is so exciting—and has become so popular—that ESPN broadcasts the daily highlights (and in some cases, lowlights) while the NFL Network broadcasts the event's entirety.

Careers are made—and lost—at the Combine.

The key word in the preceding passage is *invited*. Of all the college players hoping to turn pro each year—which we already approximated at 11,030—only about 335 receive invitations to the Combine. Getting an invite isn't just a big deal, it's the BIGGEST DEAL. That year 10 Irish players were invited to attend—a tremendous honor for any one program—and Tyreo was among them.

Unfortunately, Tyreo's Combine experience didn't go as well as we had hoped; he ran much slower than expected which I believe was attributed to the grueling demands of Combine training combined with a rigorous academic course load during Tyreo's final semester.

The good news is that Notre Dame's Pro Day—a more intimate Combine-like showcase every major Division I college holds each year for its NFL hopefuls—was a few weeks later and Tyreo would have a chance to redeem himself, at least in terms of his numerical performance. The bad news was that the weather in South Bend, Indiana on the day of the Pro Day would have made polar explorer Ernest Shackleton shiver. For the athletes taking part in the Pro Day, the frigid weather was a nonfactor—all the action took place inside Notre Dame's indoor facility. Unfortunately, agents aren't allowed inside during the workouts. While freezing my tail off, I'm running back and forth as people come out, doing my best to identify the team principals by their team paraphernalia— coats, hats, scarves, snowsuits—and present them with the marketing materials I had created on Tyreo's behalf, brochures highlighting all of Tyreo's considerable accomplishments on the field along with the many intangibles—strength of character, community service, the list goes on—that would make him an asset to any team.

I didn't notice any other agents going the Iceman route to promote their clients but, inside those walls, Tyreo was giving it everything he had and then some to make his lifelong dream come true. If I had to endure a little (or a lot of) frostbite to help make that dream become a reality, so be it.

But there was an additional benefit to being the only professional negotiator running around like a headless chicken in an industrial freezer—I was building a network. By looking those scouts, coaches and GMs in the eyes and shaking their hands, even if they never bothered to look at the handouts, I knew without question they would remember (and hopefully admire and respect) the lengths I was willing to go to promote my clients. Hopefully my frozen sweat would pay dividends on draft day. And sometimes just an extra morsel of consideration is all that's needed to turn possibility into actuality.

For Tyreo Harrison, possibility DID become actuality. He was drafted by the Philadelphia Eagles in the sixth round (198th overall). It was one of the most exhilarating moments of my life. Not just on a personal level, although I'm not going to lie, it was an incredible feeling knowing all my hard work had paid off but, bigger picture, playing a role in helping someone achieve something earth-shatteringly amazing that they've wanted since they were a child is a high unlike anything imaginable.

But in the NFL, dreams can end just as quickly as they begin. Tyreo may have been drafted by the Eagles but, for all intents and purposes, he still wasn't ON the Eagles' team—at least not in terms of the final roster.

In the offseason, NFL teams are allowed to carry a total of 90 players (recently raised from 80). By the third week of preseason, all teams must cut 15 players, bringing their total number down to 75. By the time the regular season begins, teams must reduce their numbers again, this time down to 53—45 active players allowed to dress for each game plus eight inactive players. Teams are also allowed an additional eight players for the scout team, commonly referred to as the practice squad. Players can be jockeyed back and forth throughout the season from the '53' (active or inactive), to the practice squad and back (depending on injuries, team strategies, disciplinary measures, personal issues, etc.), and are paid accordingly.

In 2013, the minimum salary for a rookie on the 53-man roster (active or inactive, it doesn't matter) was $405,000, paid over the 17 weeks of the season; just under $24K per week. However, players on the 8-man practice squad received a sizable pay cut—$5,700 per week. Please understand, just south of $6K a week is fantastic money—more than most people will ever make—but when compared to the next rung up the ladder, there's a tremendous gap. But hey, you know what they say: Membership has its privileges.

Tyreo worked his tail off in training camp, impressed all the coaches, defied the odds commonly associated with a late-round draft pick and not only made the team—he actually made the 53-man roster. He was now officially a Philadelphia Eagle.

However, just three weeks into the regular season Tyreo found himself in the National Football League's version of limbo—on waivers. In the event your copy of Webster's doesn't offer a proper definition, waivers is the NFL's labor management procedure where a team makes one of their player's contracts or rights (such as the draft rights to an unsigned player) available to every team in the league. In the off-season, teams have a few days to file a claim for a player on waivers but once the season begins, teams have just 24 hours to make a filing. If more than one team files a claim, the team with the lower winning percentage receives the assignation. If a player passes through waivers unclaimed he becomes a free agent. Worth noting: teams cannot contact players on waivers directly but must wait until that player passes waivers or is released by his current team.

One of the things I pride myself on is gathering information. Information for a sports agent is the same as ammunition for a soldier behind enemy lines—you can never have too much. For that year's draft—like any other draft—I studied every team, their current rosters, their likely returnees, and players they'd likely target with their picks. Additionally, I made it a point to know who each team's offensive and defensive coordinators were and the systems they preferred to run. Anything that could give me an edge in determining which team would be the best fit for my clients. Why? So I could concentrate my efforts pitching them and their talents to a team that might actually draft them, not a team that would ultimately have no use for them. There's not all that much time between picks—10 minutes in the first round, 7 minutes in the second, 5 minutes in rounds three through seven—and calling every team's scout, position coach, head coach or GM in that expanse is an impossibility. If you don't concentrate your efforts you—and your client—are toast.

That year, coming out of training camp the Eagles kept eight linebackers, which I thought was a bit strange considering they ran a 4-3 defense—four defensive linemen, three linebackers. Usually, teams will go two-deep at each position. So, for a 4-3 defense, that'd be two Mikes (middle linebackers), two Sams (strongside linebackers), and two Wills (weakside linebackers). But they kept eight, meaning they were three deep in two spots, so they could easily afford to get rid of one or two linebackers and still be fine—something I was keenly aware of in regard to Tyreo. Simply put, my client was expendable—yet another harsh reality of pro football.

For the first few weeks of that season the Eagles went back and forth, dealing with injuries, moving players to the inactive roster, bringing in players off the practice squad, placing guys on waivers then, once they cleared, signing them to the practice team. Then, after the third regular season game, they had an injury at another position and needed to make some room on the roster. That meant it was Tyreo's turn on the chopping-block; the intent was to place him on waivers with the hopes of resigning him to the practice squad, provided no one else claimed him.

As it turned out, nobody did claim him. However, like a squirrel before winter, I had been busy, fielding calls from other teams, talking him up a storm.

I spoke with the Minnesota Vikings; Jeff Robinson was their director of pro personnel. Reggie McKenzie called me from the Green Bay Packers. At the time, he was their pro personnel director. Now, he's the GM for the Oakland Raiders.

Reggie said, "Look, we have a kid that we drafted the year before—Torrance Marshall from Oklahoma." Kid was a stud second-round draft pick. Apparently, he was having a hard time picking up their defense—also a 4-3—where he was being groomed as the Mike (the middle linebacker). This meant he'd be making the defensive calls. However, to do that he'd have to know their defense inside and out. He was having difficulty adjusting, as many young pros do when being taught offensive or defensive schemes different than what they had run and had become accustomed to in college. But because Marshall was such a freak athlete, they couldn't imagine cutting him. Instead, they decided to move him to another position—fullback on offense. Which meant they still needed a linebacker and Tyreo was among the best available.

"I know your guy just got released," Reggie continued. "And we want to sign him. Only problem is, we can't sign him to our 53 right now."

Now Reggie is a stand-up guy. He's always been completely upfront with me and I like and respect him a lot. In addition to possessing a great football mind, he's just a great guy overall.

So Reggie explained the Torrance Marshall to fullback

scenario to me and then got into his plans for Tyreo a little further. Their current starting middle linebacker was Hardy Nickerson, a superstar household name player with 15 years in the league. The idea was to get Tyreo signed to their practice squad and get him up to speed with their playbook. Tyreo was super smart; he was Dean's List at Notre Dame—and then as soon as he learned the defense they'd pull him up to the 53 where he'd back up Hardy Nickerson. The following year, when Hardy retired, it would be Tyreo's spot to lose. Great situation.

So, I jumped on the phone with Tyreo and explained the pros and cons of both sides.

On one hand, he was familiar with the system in Philly and was already settled into a short-term apartment. But the Eagles kept eight linebackers and now it was painfully obvious Tyreo was number eight. Barring something miraculous, he'd be teetering on the edge of instability for the entire season.

On the other hand, he had a potentially plumb situation in Green Bay; I checked and rechecked the Packers roster and everything Reggie told me was spot-on. So, after weighing our options we decided Green Bay was the best scenario and I told Tyreo not to report to the Eagles facility the following day so we could let everything play out.

The next morning when Tyreo didn't show my phone blew up with frantic calls from the Eagles. Tom Heckert, their director of player personnel called me, irate. And so did head coach Andy Reid who was flat-out livid when I explained Tyreo's situation and what we had decided upon.

"You don't make a lateral move to a practice squad!" Andy screamed at me so loud I could hear his mustache hairs bristling against the phone. "Once you get level you go back to the same team; You never make a lateral move to a practice squad!"

It was nice to hear they valued Tyreo enough to fight for his services, even if they were only in the form of verbal assaults at his agent and, who knows, he may not have been in as great a demand the following week. But still, they were clearly panicked at the thought of losing him. However, that didn't change anything.

The Eagles ran a 4-3 defensive scheme and kept eight linebackers on their roster; nearly enough to field an entire third string which is unheard of in the NFL. "Look Andy, with all due respect, I'm doing what's best for my client. Look at your roster. You kept eight linebackers and my client is obviously number eight. I'd much rather put him in a position where he has a better shot of not only making the 53 but potentially rising to that of a starter and building his career long-term."

So Andy and I went back and forth for a bit, and then I called Tyreo and explained what had been said, giving him an honest relay of how upset the Eagles were, but I also reaffirmed that he should just stay home for a while and let it all play out. He had to trust me.

Shortly thereafter, Tom Heckert called me with an incredible offer—the Eagles had agreed to pay Tyreo 53-man roster money while he was on their practice squad, a difference of $9,235 more per week.

I immediately called Tyreo and explained the new scenario. I said, "Look, if the Packers are willing to commit and give us some firm commitment as to when you'd be pulled up onto their 53 that's one thing but with Philly coming with a much stronger salary, for a defense you're already familiar with, in a city and surroundings you're already settled into …"

We both agreed the right move was to stay with the Eagles. Now money isn't everything but for a rookie player, a sixth-round draft pick no less, making legit NFL 53-man roster money is nothing to sneeze at.

Tyreo spent the next four weeks on the Eagles' practice squad before being called up again to their 53, which is where he remained for the next two seasons. During that four-week period on the practice squad he earned $36,940 more than the 'usual' practice squad player did—a salary most people would be happy to earn in a year. Sure, it might have been a bit risky to rankle the feathers (pun intended) of the Eagles' coaches and management. But in situations like those, a good agent will always make it clear that his client is simply following his instructions, nothing more. Tyreo trusted me to do the best for him that I possibly could and I took that duty very seriously.

However, my favorite "going to the mat for my client" moment with Tyreo took place the following year when he was fined $5,000 for an "incident" that took place during kickoff coverage against the New England Patriots in the second game of the season.

That year, in addition to his role as a backup linebacker, Tyreo was seeing considerable special teams action. On this particular play the tackle had already been made and his teammate, Justin Ena, who became a very close friend of his, was on the ground, prone on his back. One of the Patriots was on top of Justin, shoving his helmet into the ground.

Tyreo saw this, ran over and knocked the Patriot player off. There was no tackle, no sustained contact, just a quick shove, a helping hand down to his teammate and that was it. Yes, there was contact with an opposing player after the whistle had blown which was a flaggable offense, however; in this case, the crime was worth the punishment.

Justin and Tyreo trotted off the field, back to their sideline. There were no words exchanged, no standing over the guy to intimidate, just a bang-bang play. However, the ref did throw a flag, calling a personal foul for Unnecessary Roughness, and tacked on 15 yards to the Patriots' kick return. After the game—I think it was later in the week—Tyreo was notified by Gene Washington in the league office that he would be fined $5,000 for the infraction, the money to be taken from his game check.

Now $5,000 is still $5,000, no matter if you earn $100,000 a year or $100 million. In this case, $5,000 was no tiny amount. But the fine represented more than just a monetary penalty—it was the principle. Tyreo had done what any other team-conscious player would do in that situation—come to the aid of a teammate—and done the absolute minimum—just what was necessary—to extricate his teammate from the predicament he was in (albeit, I did have the benefit of video replay to aid my analysis, whereas the referee did not).

When Tyreo called and told me he'd been fined, I immediately said we should appeal it. He had told me exactly what happened that day on the field and, knowing his character, knowing he was honest to a fault and wouldn't embellish the story to make himself look better or his position more righteous, I knew in my heart that we had to appeal it.

At first, he wasn't keen on the idea. Not only didn't he want to make waves, but also he said the veteran players all told him just to forget about it. They told him that that no one ever won their appeal against a $5,000 Unnecessary Roughness fine.

But this is where that supreme player-agent trust comes in. If you're not on the same page for matters such as this, the relationship can't work. First, I stated the obvious, that $5,000, at that stage of his career, wasn't chump change. In my eyes—and I think in the eyes of most people—what Tyreo did was admirable. He took swift action—without overdoing it—trying to prevent a teammate from getting hurt. What's more, if any fine was to be handed out, it should have gone to the Patriots player who was shoving Justin Ena's helmet into the turf.

Again, Tyreo brought up the fact that his veteran teammates uniformly said that his chances of winning the appeal were slimmer than slim. Maybe, if the stars were in alignment and the football gods were feeling charitable the fine would be reduced slightly, but it certainly wouldn't be done away with. No chance. So don't bother wasting your time, especially not for $5,000.

Still, I couldn't let it go. The frugal side of me wanted to protect every penny any of my clients earned. But the moral side of me didn't want Tyreo thinking he'd done something wrong, something that wasn't honorable, something that a good teammate wouldn't do. Therefore, after a bit more conversation it was agreed that we would appeal the fine and I sent notice to the league office of our intent to do just that.

The hearing took place about four weeks later by teleconference; we'd be speaking with three-time Super Bowl champion and NFL Hall of Famer Art Shell, at the time the Senior Vice President of the league, in charge of football operations.

Prior to the teleconference, the league sent me a video of the game. Even though it was 2003 everything was still old school—they sent me a VHS. I watched the play in question over and over and made my analysis. My argument was that Tyreo's actions were crystal clear. There was no prolonged or sustained contact. Just the initial impact to knock the Patriots player off his downed teammate and that was the end of it. No secondary taunting, threatening gestures, follow-up contact— nothing. It was bang-bang and over.

Then, in addition to my analysis of the play, itself, which I prepared in an organized collection of notes just as if I were going to trial, I composed additional notes to bolster my argument. For example, Tyreo is not nor has ever been considered a dirty player. Also, on that occasion, there was no intent to injure the other player, only to prevent the injury to his own teammate. But I didn't stop there. I went so far as to compile evidence from Tyreo's college career at Notre Dame; not once had he been flagged for unnecessary roughness or unsportsmanlike conduct. He was simply a player who played within the rules, hard but fair, and never demonstrated intent to injure anyone.

I drafted and Tyreo signed a character affidavit attesting to that fact, rolling out his past like a red carpet. Tyreo's character, especially the character he'd exhibited as a player in a big-time program like Notre Dame, was beyond reproach. I even drafted an affidavit for myself, as an attorney admitted to the Bar of New York State. That, as Tyreo's agent, having known him for three years, knowing him to be a former Dean's List student at Notre Dame, knowing everything he had done for his community, I knew firsthand that his character was without flaws.

But I didn't stop there. Remember what I said about never having too much information?

I reached out to the NFL Players Association and asked for statistics from the previous year looking for not only reductions in fines, but full rescissions. The NFLPA takes great pride in their work and I quickly received a list of every player that had been fined the previous year with all the relevant data: game, player, type of infraction, amount of the fine, you name it. I scanned the list looking for similar fines to what Tyreo had been cited for—Unnecessary Roughness—then looked for rescissions for the same fine amount. I found one, Brad Scioli, a defensive tackle for the Indianapolis Colts. He received a $5,000 fine for administering a hit that drew a flag for Unnecessary Roughness and a 15-yard penalty, and the fine was completely rescinded.

Bingo! Now I had precedent on my side, as well—a completely meritless fine that was appealed and overturned. I was ecstatic. And I was ready to do battle on behalf of my client.

So Tuesday rolls around—the typical day off for NFL teams and players—the teleconference kicks off and I lay it all out. I'm in my New York office. Art Shell was in the NFL office, also in New York, on Park Avenue. And Tyreo was down in Philly.

After some no-nonsense introductory pleasantries, Art said something to the effect of, "Alright, say your piece because I'm watching the video." So I launched into my spiel, going through every note I had made, every piece of information and evidence I had compiled. I presented—*Tyreo's case*—in the most compelling way I possibly could. Succinct but with a savvy trial lawyer's cadence. After all, I didn't want to put the guy to sleep.

When it was over Art signed off short and sweet. "Okay. Thank you. I'm going to take this under advisement. I'll let you know what I decide."

When the conference call ended I felt as I did after the Bar exam. I knew I had prepared to the best of my ability, dotting all the i's, crossing all the t's. I believed in my heart of hearts that I hadn't left a single stone unturned. Not one. And to be perfectly honest I felt the odds were in our favor. That's not me being cocky, or overconfident. I was just very at peace with all that had transpired. It was part faith, and also that we had gone above and beyond what normal people would do to defend a principle that was worth defending. But that's how I approach every aspect of my business. Above and beyond. Whatever it takes.

However, aside from his short statement at the beginning of the call, Art didn't really say much of anything, leaving Tyreo and I in the dark about what had just happened and, more important, where we stood with the fine.

"You know what I think he was doing?" Tyreo said with a chuckle. "I think he was checking his stocks the entire time."

We both started laughing. "You might be right," I said. "I could totally see him checking his portfolio."

"Hey man, I appreciate you trying," he said. "That's what I'm here for," I said. "That's what I'll always be here for." Two weeks later Tyreo called me ecstatic. "You did it! You did it!" he roared. "I got the letter from the league. They rescinded the entire fine!" A day later I received a copy of that same letter from Art Shell. He referenced every single point I made as a reason for rescinding the fine. Apparently he wasn't monitoring his stock portfolio!

While Tyreo and I already had a cement-like bond—the same bond I strive for with all my clients—that event strengthened it even further. It confirmed to Tyreo—and my other clients who got wind of our victory—that not only was I someone they could trust, but I also had the expertise, the knowledge and the tenacity to go above and beyond, to do whatever it took to defend their rights and interests to the fullest. This wasn't just their job, this wasn't just their dream—

this was their life. Their everything. And their everything is certainly worth my everything. I am my brother's keeper.

Chapter 1

· ·

Hall of Fame Roots

"Blood is thicker than water."
~ *Peter W. Lee*

Thanks to movies like *Jerry Maguire* and *Million Dollar Arm* and shows like *Arli$$* player representation is seen by many as, well, sexy. At a cocktail party, when you tell people you're a sports agent, they naturally want to hear more about it. In reality, player representation is somewhere on the continuum between sexy and the scene in *Jerry Maguire* where Jerry tells Rod, in a moment of exasperated candor, "It's a pride-swallowing siege which I will never fully tell you about."

It is, in reality, car rental counters and Holiday Inns, more than it is limousines and The Four Seasons. It is profit and loss. It is explaining to your wife why you need to rent a car and drive to Akron through a monsoon in order to be with a prospect you may not even sign. It is taking care of the lives and finances and dreams of young people, while also trying to make a living. It is the continuous (and tenuous) management of your own dreams. It is the audacious belief that you can do something unique and lasting, even though all of the signs

1

point elsewhere.

Destiny. Fate. Kismet. Call it what you will, but growing up in the shadow of the Pro Football Hall of Fame in Canton, OH the stars must've been aligned in the shape of a one-hundred-yard gridiron pointing both west to Notre Dame and east to New York City. It must've been cosmic force that prompted me to leave the security of a cushy job at a top NYC law firm to pursue a career in one of, if not THE, most cutthroat industry in the world—the business of NFL player representation. However, as I've come to realize over the past few years, my path was already chosen for me.

Confidence was instilled and ingrained in me by my parents at a very young age. My parents were wonderful, loving role models who taught my brother and me—through their own tireless example—about discipline, drive, perseverance, sacrifice and selfless love. About going above and beyond in every instance to do whatever it takes to finish the job to the best of your ability. If I ever brought home a B+ on my report card in grade school, my Dad would calmly tell me "if this were your best, we would be happy with it, but we both know, it is not your best" … and I knew that to be true as well.

My parents taught me to never sell myself short in any endeavor—no matter how big or small—to expect and deliver only the absolute best I had to give. To live relentless and leave nothing on the table. I learned early on, the defining mantra of my life—that you reap what you sow. This principle manifested itself in my drive to become one of the best, if not the best, basketball player in the junior high parochial league. I spent countless hours under the scorching summer sun shooting baskets at the hoop in my parents' driveway and was able to parlay my methodically honed skill set to two championship game appearances for the St. Michael Vikings. From this loving foundation of steadfast support, my brother and I grew to believe that we could achieve anything in this world—that if we dreamed it, it was indeed possible. Whether it was to be a professional quarterback, the first Korean-American point guard in the NBA, or a corporate lawyer spearheading multi-billion dollar mergers and acquisitions, my parents engendered in me the confidence, work ethic and hunger to achieve my dreams.

My early childhood dreams were not on the gridiron, however. They were more of the Paul Simon/Bob Dylan variety. Every time my parents would throw dinner parties at our house, my chutzpah would manifest itself when I would get up in front of the adults and sing and perform with my little toy guitar. To this day, I remember one song in particular (describing the ultimate sadness of saying good-bye to a friend who had come over to play) whose lyrics went something like this: "And I say, Mommy, let him stay, or let her stay, but you say no, just play with toys!" (Heavy metal strumming ensues).

Sometimes, pitching a prospect's family feels a lot like singing before strangers did. It's never easy saying good-bye to a recruit who has decided to go in a different direction; especially when you have invested so much of your time, energy and passion in developing the relationship.

Growing up as a Korean-American boy in Canton, OH in the mid-70s and 80s, I never really had to deal with the scourge of uninformed racism. I credit my parents for a lot of that because I never grew up trying to fit myself into a neat little box whether it was being Korean-American, Catholic, or a Pittsburgh Steelers fan (yes, I grew up rooting for the Black and Gold in Cleveland Browns Country). Instead, I wanted people to know, understand, appreciate and respect me on my own terms, for my own personality, my own qualifications, my own character, and not for the color of my skin. Over the years, I have come to understand that this viewpoint—as espoused by the late Dr. Martin Luther King, Jr.—is the open-minded, loving ideal for which wars are continually fought and lives are lost…and yet the same ideal that justifies the ultimate sacrifice given in its pursuit.

Having come to grips with my own defining character traits at a relatively young age, I came to understand that being on the losing side was one place where I did NOT want to be. Whether it was a family Monopoly game or schoolyard football game, my competitive fire raged bright and deep within. I abhorred losing, but it was through these failures that my character was molded to prepare for the success that was about to come.

Having not been chosen for the Canton North Avondale traveling hot stove team in fifth grade (while all of my best friends made the team), I rebounded and stayed locked in all season long in the non-traveling league to help lead our team to the championship game. As the third baseman and closer for our team, I had pitched the day before to seal our victory in the semifinal and came down with a serious (for an eleven-year-old) case of elbow tendonitis the night before the championship game. I vividly remember my dad trying out his home remedy and slathering my arm with Ben Gay with Saran Wrap wrapped around before going to bed that evening. Remarkably, the arm felt decent enough and I was able to play the next day. I knew, in that moment, that my father loved me and that in spite of all that he had going on in his life (which included the application for six US patents related to roller bearing design and function), he truly cared. That is one of my enduring memories of my father and one of the things I have tried to carry with me into my agency—the idea that caring for the athlete must be my primary concern.

We were up 3-2 in the bottom of the ninth and I was brought in to close the game. After striking out the first two batters, I took the third batter to a 3-2 count before walking him. I then proceeded to hit the next batter and walk the subsequent one. With the bases loaded, I forced a weak groundball that dribbled through our first baseman's legs (the pre-Bill Buckner). Two runs scored and we ended up losing the game. I was absolutely devastated and remember collapsing to the mound trying to shield my tears from view. After the sting of defeat wore off, we picked up our trophies and headed out for ice cream—everyone that is, except for me. I ended up going home—not wanting to be around anyone, but wanting only to sit in my room, wallow in my defeat and let it all sink in (which I did for the next few hours).

Without saying a word, my Dad understood and did not force me to go with the team for ice cream. To this day, that meant the world to me. Over the years, I have gotten much better at accepting the inevitable defeats, but the importance of investing and committing every ounce of my body, heart and soul to "climb the mountain" so that there are absolutely no regrets in the pursuit of victory is an invaluable life lesson that I learned through the losses of my childhood and the only solace I could ever find in defeat. And losing still stings. I feel it every time I pour my heart and soul into a prospective client who signs elsewhere. It happens in the business, but has still provided many "dark nights of the soul."

Sports were my passion as a child, but the principles of teamwork and fun also applied to something more nostalgic and old-school such as learning how to build a fire, tie a good knot and do a good deed. So, at the urging of my parents, I joined Cub Scouts (Pack 122) and then matriculated to Boy Scouts (Troop 122) at St. Michael's School.

I absolutely loved Boy Scouts. However, the one memory seared in my mind is that of our troop's summer trip to Massachusetts in 1986. The outlook was bright when we departed on a sunny Saturday morning for Miles Standish State Park. We had a caravan of station wagons, trucks and a small trailer (newly constructed by the elders of Troop 122) to hold all of our camping gear. The 12 hour drive went by rather quickly and we set up camp that evening. It turns out that the uneventful drive out ended up being the highlight of the trip. It poured the entire time we were in Massachusetts—literally 6 out of 7 days—and our tents became so waterlogged that they began to cave in and flood. We ended up sleeping for a majority of the trip in seats of station wagons and trucks. The latrines stank to high heaven and, for whatever reason our troop leaders thought it was a good idea for us to make a day trip to Provincetown on Cape Cod, where many of us experienced firsthand for the first time open "alternative" living. After having slogged through enough rain to sustain an entire season's harvest, we ended up leaving for Ohio on a Saturday evening and it was during our nighttime ride that the tire on our homemade trailer blew on the Pennsylvania Turnpike. It was while we were waiting to find a replacement tire at a gas station near Lewisburg, PA that we heard over the radio that two convicts had escaped from the nearby maximum security penitentiary and were considered armed and dangerous. As I peered around and saw the concerned looks on our adult leaders' faces, I found a weird sense of peace in knowing that everything was going to be alright—having hit rock bottom, I knew there was no place to go but up. Luckily, we made it home without incident early the next morning. Having raised two Eagle Scouts meant the world to my father and we had the privilege of placing our Eagle Scout pins in his casket when he passed in 2001.

I realize now that my brother and I were truly blessed to have the parents we had. Parents who would always subordinate themselves and put their kids first in anything, making them the priority, and supporting them in any way that they could—financially, emotionally, intellectually and spiritually. Parents who instilled in us the confidence to know that we could achieve anything we set out to do if we worked hard, believed in ourselves and kept our faith in God. Their unconditional love and selfless sacrifice still inspire and motivate me to this day. Strength comes from God, but inspiration is the appreciation for everything that my mother and father sacrificed to help support us in our dreams.

My Dad and Mom migrated to the United States in the early 1960s. They met in Milwaukee at a Korean Student Association dance while my Dad attended Marquette (while loading trucks for UPS at night) and my Mom attended the University of Wisconsin-Milwaukee. At the time, I had no idea the sacrifice my dad was making for us. I knew he was brilliant, and worked with his mind…but now it means the world to me that he would leave home in the middle of the night to go and grind away with his body. I hope and pray that I have inherited even a fraction of his work ethic.

After a brief courtship, my Dad and Mom decided to get married and sent out their engagement notices on April 1, 1967. Having no knowledge of April Fool's Day, Dad and Mom had no idea why so many of their friends kept calling to ask them if the engagement was a joke!

Mom was and still is a superwoman. After my brother entered school, Mom went back to work at the US Post Office in Akron, OH. She worked nights which meant that her workweek consisted of getting home at 7:15a.m., cooking a quick breakfast for my Dad, me and my brother and then seeing us off to work and school. Mom would then take a nap until noon, clean the house and do laundry and welcome us home from school with an after school snack. She would end her marathon day by cooking dinner for my Dad, me and my brother and then taking another nap from 7:00p.m. to 9:00p.m. before rising to leave for the post office at 9:45p.m. Mom did this every night for 15 years and not once did I ever hear her complain. The sacrifice she made for her boys and husband left an indelible mark on my soul and heart

Mom would always say "When you work, work hard. When you play, play hard," and she lived this aphorism with a vibrant sense of humor and thirst for life. As an agent, it's often hard to leave work at the office, as you are often on call 24/7 for clients. But a healthy balance and perspective is beneficial not only for me, but for my clients. Our culture makes an idol of football, and while we work as hard as we can, we don't want to do the same.

In addition to the "unique" sense of humor and joie de vivre that Mom has imparted to me, I have learned from her own poignant example the importance of persevering and moving forward through the inevitable obstacles, setbacks and hardships of life. One of the hardest feelings and moments of my life was on the Monday morning when my mom left after visiting me in NYC for her birthday one month after my dad died. As she waved good-bye and got into a taxi headed for LaGuardia, I could see she was crying a little bit. I knew she had to go back to Ohio to face the harsh reality that she was by herself now. It just tore at my heart. But, Mom is a trooper, a complete trooper. And from the vibrant way she has lived her life in the fourteen years since my father passed, I know that the show must go on.

Dad was the best man I have ever known. He was a brilliant man—with a PhD in metallurgical engineering and 6 US patents and 2 European patents to his name—with an off-the-charts work ethic who lived his life selflessly for his family and others. Dad earned a bachelor's degree in mechanical engineering from Seoul National University—South Korea's version of Harvard—but, since his overseas degree was not honored in the United States, he ended up earning another bachelor's degree at Marquette University before going on to earn his master's and PhD at Drexel University. Yet, despite his brilliance, Dad never brought work home. He was simply Dad. He lived for his kids and wife and immersed himself into our lives and activities. Dad didn't know how to swim, yet he taught us how to do so through private lessons. He didn't know how to ride a bike, yet he taught my brother and me how to ride our Schwinns as soon as we entered kindergarten. Dad never went on a campout, yet he became an assistant scoutmaster and was instrumental in supporting my brother and me in our journey to the rank of Eagle Scout. Dad never played baseball, yet he was our assistant little league baseball coach and spent countless hours catching for me in the backyard in my days as a young Goose Gossage.

What I admired most about Dad was his innate humility and never-ending journey toward personal and spiritual growth—a journey that did not end until he took his last breath on this Earth. Coming from an educated family in South Korea (where my grandfather was a high-ranking politician), Dad was raised in a caste system that celebrated education and socioeconomic rank and looked down upon those who earned their living through manual labor and industrial trades. When he migrated to the United States in the early 1960s, he brought with him that very same mindset that was ingrained in him from his youth. However, over the years, as he grew to know and respect stellar men and women from all different walks of life, Dad had the open-mindedness and courage to reevaluate, question and ultimately refute the flawed cultural ideology that was programmed in him from so long ago. He learned to appreciate and love people based on their character alone.

That is a lesson often directly at odds with the prevailing culture in professional sports—where seeing people as dollar signs, and using them accordingly is commonplace. Without my dad's example, I'm not sure I could survive this business with my integrity intact.

Dad's calling hours only served to reinforce this truth. The calling hours took place in blizzard-like conditions on a Monday evening in early March. Seeing dear friends who loved my father—from all different walks of life and educational and socioeconomic backgrounds—moved me to tears. You had janitors and medical doctors, whites, blacks and Asians, young and old alike who had braved the hazardous conditions to pay their respects to my Dad. I remember a big, burly physical therapist who had worked with my Dad a year before during rehab from a mild stroke crying to me while saying "I learned more from your father in one month than I could've ever taught him." My Dad's dear friend Jack Harrison was there as well. Jack Harrison was an ex-Navy veteran who was the scoutmaster for our Cub Scout pack. My Dad met Jack when I had first signed up for Cub Scouts more than twenty years ago, and from there, an unexpected friendship developed. Jack never met a curse word he didn't like (fitting for a sailor) while my Dad hardly ever cursed (I never heard him ever drop the F bomb and only once or twice heard him say BS). Jack was blue-collar through and through while my Dad was a brilliant intellectual who had more years of academia than any man I had ever known. Yet at their core, they were great men—and through it all, their friendship endured and deepened over the years; to the point where I saw Jack Harrison bawling like a baby at my Dad's calling hours saying to me repeatedly "Your Dad was my best friend." Seeing this type of love and brotherhood left a profound impact on my soul. You judge a man by character and character alone. There is no status based on wealth, fame or education in the eyes of God.

My Dad had touched so many lives during his brief time on Earth, yet I live my life, and my brother does as well, to ensure that his legacy lives on through the lives we continue to touch. As Billy Joel once said, "Only the good die young."

It was my Dad and Mom's long-term vision for my future that prompted them to urge (well, force) me to take the road less traveled before my freshman year of high school. It was a monumental, life-changing decision that positively altered the course of my life.

Having graduated from eighth grade at St. Michael's School, I was set up very nicely to attend our feeder high school, Canton Central Catholic. As class president and a rising basketball star, I was poised to be the man, the BMOC, my freshman year at Central (as much as one can be a BMOC as a freshman)….until my parents dropped the bomb on me that July. They wanted me to attend GlenOak High School (the public high school in our school district). I was absolutely dumbfounded, upset and angry all at the same time. I did not want to go. I felt that all of the groundwork I had laid over the past eight years in setting myself up for a seamless transition to our Catholic feeder high school was all for naught. My fear was that of the unknown—of having to start all over again in making new friends and establishing my identity as a leader, an intellect and an athlete. It was the most daunting fear I had experienced in my life up to that point. Walking through the doors of a large, loud, and foreign public high school on the first day was indeed terrifying. Not unlike walking through the heavy, intimidating doors of an NFL facility to negotiate my first player contract. These minor and momentary afflictions were preparing me for something greater.

As often was the case, Mom and Dad knew best. In hindsight, attending GlenOak High School was the absolute best decision I could've ever made (or my parents could've made for me). Number one, it toughened me up. I knew that I had to work my tail off to establish myself socially, academically and athletically and that the comfort and shelter of a private school education would be no more. Number two, I developed some great core friends; dear friends of mine even to this day. Most important, I saw a true cross-section of society. My high school encompassed a huge school district. We drew from every demographic in a United States Census. We had kids from very affluent areas. We had kids from the projects. We had preppy kids, burnouts, terrific athletes and even the occasional celebrity (i.e., Marilyn Manson).

It was just a beautiful cross-section of society. Riding the bus my freshman and sophomore year, my bus route took us through Hills & Dales, which was arguably Canton's most affluent area at the time—a neighborhood filled with McMansions, Mercedes-Benz, and manicured lawns. However, once basketball season started, I would also drop off teammates of mine after practice in the projects on the Northeast side in the midst of liquor stores and hubcap joints.

My time at GlenOak gave me an accurate sense of what the real world is all about. I learned (and lived) that regardless of the color of your skin, the dollars in your bank account, the clothes that you wear and the house where you live, you look to the core of a human being in order to find out who they are and what they stand for. My GlenOak education served me well.

Being armed with an invaluable real-world perspective, I was now ready to conquer the world (or so I thought). But first, I needed to figure out the path I was destined to take. Fortunately, my early childhood and grade school memories offered me some helpful hints of the future that was yet to unfold.

I've always stood up for the weak and the outcast. Without any care as to what was "cool," during my fourth-grade year, I would share my seat on the school bus with Steve R (a couple years older than I, but picked on for his bookish demeanor by his peers). As an altar boy at St. Michael's, my last name happened to be sandwiched right in between Eddie M and Brian K, two of the more misunderstood, socially outcast boys in my grade. As my altar boy partners, I established friendships with both Eddie and Brian and spent time over at their houses including overnight stays. I appreciated and liked them for who they were, not for how they were viewed in the grade school court of popular opinion; whose verdict of "not cool enough" was one that I would fervently appeal. The NFL court of public opinion is not all that different. Sometimes, practically, this means recruiting the player who has flown under everyone's radar or…more likely, not recruiting the popular player who you know is not the right fit.

However, my most poignant example of brotherly love occurred during the 1987 Final Four. I had my best friend over to watch the semifinals (it was the Final Four capped by Keith Smart's game winning jumper against Syracuse). While we settled in to watch Providence vs. Syracuse, my best friend began horsing around with my younger brother, when my younger brother accidentally punched him in the nuts. My buddy was hurt, upset and angry—and despite the four-year age difference—lashed out at my brother and drove his head into the concrete floor of our basement. My attention was diverted from the game as I watched everything develop. As soon as I saw my brother begin to cry, I reacted instinctively without a second thought. I confronted my best friend and proceeded to put him in a headlock that cut his mouth badly due to his braces. He was digging his nails into my side, but I wouldn't let go. When I finally released my grasp, his mouth was bloody and he was crying, but my brother had stopped. We eventually mended our friendship, but the fight marked a watershed moment within my family. For it was then, at that very moment, my brother knew I would defend him till the day I die—that I would always be there for him to look after him and protect him; that I would always be my brother's keeper.

Chapter 2

. . . .

Going Pro

"If I have seen further, it is by standing on the shoulders of giants."

~ Sir Isaac Newton

Everything works out according to God's plan. That is my irrefutable truth and one that manifested itself during my unexpected, yet preordained, journey to the University of Notre Dame.

I fell victim to a strong case of overconfidence coming out of GlenOak High School. I had thought that with my GPA, extracurricular activities, SAT score and leadership roles that I was a shoo-in to be accepted to either Harvard, Yale or Princeton. I felt so sure of my chances that I applied to these three colleges with only one backup school, The Ohio State University, as my in state safety net. However, God has a way of humbling people and such was the case with me. I did not get in to any of my top three choices. I was devastated; however, after coming to grips with the situation, I picked myself up, dusted myself off and began preparations to attend Ohio State. It was around that time (in early May 1991) that my Dad—on a whim—called the Director of Admissions at the University of Notre Dame and inquired about submitting a late application for admission. The admissions director told my father that he couldn't promise him anything, but to go ahead and submit my application. We did, and when I received word a few days later that I had been accepted to Notre Dame, it became crystal clear to me that my last-minute admission to a top 25 school involved some divine intervention. My inconceivable journey to the Golden Dome was a sign from God ... and would ultimately change my life forever.

South Bend, Indiana, on the surface, seems a million miles away from the Ivy League. It's a small, blue-collar Midwestern town of strip malls and empty factories...except for the few square miles of well-funded utopia that comprises the Notre Dame campus.

As I began my freshman year at Notre Dame, I couldn't help but carry with me an empty feeling of loss and disappointment; the feeling that I had let myself and my loved ones down by not being good enough to gain admission to top Ivy League schools. Gradually, as I immersed myself into the Notre Dame culture, this vacuous feeling began to dissipate. The watershed moment for me was walking back to my dorm on the south quad after a workout at "The Rock" (the Rockne Memorial Gym) on a crisp, cool fall evening with the quad lights illuminating the way. As I glanced up to the sky, I saw countless stars dotting the heavens with the light from the Golden Dome refracting in the corner of my eye. At that moment, there was no regret over what could or should have been. There was only hope and elation for what would be. A cleansing peace washed over me and I knew right then and there that Notre Dame was where I was meant to be—

and I committed myself to making the most of the experience. Apart from the academic coursework, I was the recipient of higher education on the courts and fields of competition as well. I took a crash course during freshman orientation weekend. I remember playing horse with LaRon Moore, a freshman wide receiver from Indianapolis, and being amazed by his basketball skill set. LaRon was so fast and quick and had a 40" vertical leap to boot, but he could also shoot, handle and pass the ball…which was totally unfair considering basketball wasn't even his sport! One of my dorm mates in Alumni Hall was Steve Verduzco, a freshman shortstop on the baseball team. Steve decided to attend Notre Dame on a full-ride despite being selected in the fifth round by the Philadelphia Phillies the year before and was a 6'1" 200 lb. athlete with 4.5 speed. Walking on south quad that weekend, I ran into one of the largest, most athletic looking men I had ever seen, Oscar McBride, a backup tight end on the football team who would go on to play in the NFL. Oscar was a kindhearted soul who also happened to look like a power forward—6'6" 255 lbs. of lean muscle. It was right around this time that I began to realize that I was no longer in Kansas anymore.

Superior athleticism was prevalent everywhere you looked on campus. It manifested itself in the greatest college football recruiting class in history—Notre Dame's Class of 1994 (one year before my arrival). This recruiting class contained 5 NFL first round picks including Bryant Young, Aaron Taylor, Jerome Bettis, Tom Carter and Jeff Burris as well as 14 players who ended up playing in the NFL. Before he became "The Bus" and a Pro Football Hall of Fame inductee, Jerome Bettis was JB and a friend of mine. Jerome lived in my dorm and was a jovial, kindhearted soul. He was a huge man who rode around campus on a rickety ten-speed bike that was built for someone half his size (an image that endures to this day). I will never forget Jerome's kindness and unselfish spirit when he welcomed my younger brother (who also played fullback in high school) into his dorm room after the Navy game in November 1991 and took a photo with him. Jerome later autographed the photo ("To David, keep working hard and one day you will fill my shoes") and the framed photo still sits atop my brother's bookshelf in his home office.

These times hanging out with JB at Notre Dame served the twofold purpose of both solidifying my admiration for elite athletes, and also demystifying them to a large degree. I saw the pain that JB played through…the cuts, the bruises, the injuries, and the sacrifices. But I also enjoyed him as a person, over and above what he did or didn't do on Saturday afternoons. I didn't know it at the time, but through my interactions with JB and the rest of my NFL classmates, I was being prepared for my future career.

I ran countless hours of pickup basketball games at The Rock during my freshman year and had the privilege of playing with and against Monty Williams, former NBA player and former head coach of the NBA's New Orleans Pelicans. Monty was forced to sit out that season due to an irregular heartbeat (it was one year after the Hank Gathers tragedy so team doctors were definitely erring on the side of caution) and they would have blown a gasket had they known that Monty was playing pickup ball every afternoon and evening at The Rock. Now, I had been a good high school basketball player and a decent athlete, but I had never before experienced this level of freakish athleticism and ability. Monty was a 6'8" athlete with point guard handle, NBA three-point range, superior vision and passing ability and explosive hops. Playing against him was mesmerizing and sobering at the same time, but it taught me the invaluable lesson of competing against a superior opponent, where I could not rely on talent alone. I read a recent article in Sports Illustrated about the tragic suicide of Gia Allemande, the former Bachelor contestant and girlfriend of New Orleans Pelicans player Ryan Anderson, and it made me proud to learn about how Monty and his wife, as devout Christians, were there for Ryan and prayed with him that fateful evening. Although it's been more than twenty years since those pickup games at The Rock, I was so proud of my Notre Dame brother and the man he had become.

**

My knees are bleeding. Bending over in exhaustion, my cotton T-shirt soaked with sweat, I'm battling it out with my pickup basketball team on the blacktop behind Hammes Bookstore in South Bend. The Bookstore Basketball tournament is an annual rite of passage at Notre Dame. Bookstore Basketball is the world's largest five-on-five basketball tournament with more than 700 teams entered to participate each year. Each team is required to have a name and scandalous creativity is always on display. From Malicious Prosecution (the law school team) to Four Musty Pelts and a Summer's Eve, pushing the envelope with borderline libelous names was a time-honored tradition that was almost as fun as playing the games themselves.

I'm a freshman—an undersized Asian-American from Canton, banging for rebounds against tall white kids from the basketball-crazy cornfields of Indiana, and inner-city kids from Indianapolis, Fort Wayne, and Muncie. Even at the tender age of 18 the tournament was a study in team-building and courage. I spent the weeks leading up to the tournament pitching and selling in dorm rooms and classrooms, trying to compile the kind of talent that would take us deep into the tournament.

I sacrificed my body all over the blacktop court—diving for loose balls, taking charges, playing man up pressure defense the entire court—and when it was all said and done, although we had narrowly lost the game, I felt that I had won the war. I left everything I had on the court as I crawled off in complete exhaustion on bloody knees having competed at the highest level and given my absolute best. I would need that kind of fortitude when I finally went into the agent business. There are many days where it seems too hard. When clients leave for no reason, or competitors try to damage your reputation and good name. It's easy to want to quit. But part of my admiration for the athletes I represent is that they don't quit. Day after day, no matter how much it hurts, they go back out and compete. They have their teammates' backs.

**

Starting Notre Dame linebacker Demetrius DuBose loomed large on campus—both literally and figuratively. Dubose was 6'2" and 235 pounds, and figured to be a high NFL draft choice. His dark skin and muscular physique just made him that much more intimidating, so when he approached me through a classmate—a fast talking Chicagoan whose father was a city alderman well-acquainted with questionable practices—I fell for the pyramid marketing scam hook line and sinker.

The short version is that DuBose's little syndicate briefly absconded with 100 of my hard-earned college student dollars, which I eventually got back. They also bilked me out of the several days I spent skipping class so that I could "sell" many of my friends on contributing money to the scheme.

Looking back, what the incident illustrated was the seductive and charismatic power of the high-profile athlete. People were literally forking over their money just to be near DuBose and be a part of his "foolproof" scheme. It was a dynamic that I have seen play out many times since as a sports agent. There are so many people in this business who lack a fundamental self-respect, and who must resort to paying athletes to gain their trust. I may have fallen for Dubose's scheme...but I was determined to play by another set of rules. There would be no "get rich quick" schemes for me in my career as an NFL agent. I would build my agency on a foundation of hard work, creativity and technical expertise.

My sophomore roommate was Greg Stec, a nose tackle turned center from Chicago who was arguably the toughest guy in school. He creatively dismantled our loft in Alumni Hall at the end of my sophomore year. Greg and I were unable to take apart the wooden loft by conventional means because we had expedited the process of building the loft by *hammering* in 6 inch screws back in the fall (probably not the smartest idea). With the end of the school year fast approaching, we had to look to alternate methods of destroying the loft instead.

I went out that night and ended up crashing at a buddy's place. When I came home the next morning, I found wooden shards and 2x4 splinters of what had once been the loft strewn across the room and in the hallway along with a skid-marked pair of tighty whiteys on the floor. Based on my serious sleuthing skills, my conclusion was that Greg finally got fed up and angry, and began hammering and using every ounce of energy he had to punish, destroy and annihilate the loft. Once his mission was accomplished, Greg then took a quick shower (thus, the tighty whiteys on the floor) and headed out to the bars. When I met up with Greg later that day, my hypothesis was confirmed. To this day, the destruction of that loft remains one of the most impressive feats of strength and madness that I have ever seen. The epilogue to the story—as final room inspections approached, Greg and I were both sweating it out, trying to figure out a way to patch up the massive hole in our ceiling. Greg reassured me that he was up to the task. He would head back to Chicago and bring back some "Bondo" to patch up the hole with some wet newspaper filling thrown in. I trusted Greg (I mean, how could I not after the loft demolition?) and sure enough Greg did bring back some "Bondo" from Chicago the weekend before finals week.

After taking my first final, I came back to the room and noticed a sagging crater where the hole in our ceiling used to be. It was a heroic effort on Greg's part, but it was one of the worst patch up jobs I had ever seen. The wet newspaper filling was apparently too heavy for the exterior resin and the weight was causing the putty to sag and droop. When the room inspector came, I stayed right in front of his face, talking actively and directing him around very quickly from space to space. Luckily for us, the inspector never looked up at the ceiling and the makeshift repair job passed muster, thus, bringing to an end the saga of the unbreakable loft.

Having grown intellectually, athletically, spiritually and socially from immersing myself into the full college experience, it was quite fitting that my future career path was paved on the hardwood courts at Notre Dame. After graduating with my undergraduate degree in Accountancy, *summa cum laude*, in May 1995, I began attending Notre Dame

Law School that fall. Although the coursework and study demands of law school were much more rigorous than undergrad (we were told during orientation that in the first year of law school, they scare you to death, in the second year, they work you to death, and in the third year, they bore you to death—frighteningly accurate, btw), I still made it a priority to workout daily and release some steam. My competitive fire still burned brightly and I became a regular at Rolfs (the student rec center) where I played pickup games with undergraduate students including varsity football players during the off-season. As time passed and I began to gain respect for my decent "law school game," I started to develop friendships with several of these players. Players such as Lamont Bryant, one of my first and all-time favorite clients and a brother from another mother.

Lamont was a starting defensive end and a tremendous natural athlete. Anthony Denman, All-American linebacker and another future client (and no athletic slouch in his own right), told me when he arrived at Notre Dame as a freshman running back from Texas, he simply stood in awe (and a little bit of fear) as Lamont walked the entire length of the football field...on his hands!

"Eugene," he said one day after we sucked down a post-workout Gatorade. "You should think about getting your certification and representing me." I was intrigued. What's more, it proved the importance of relationships in the business, that Lamont was ready to put his professional future in the hands of, basically, a peer. But this is how one of the NFL's first super agents, Leigh Steinberg, got his start—as a classmate of quarterback Steve Bartkowski at Cal.

As our friendships developed, a couple of other players asked me to apply for my certification through the NFLPA.

They already knew that I had accepted a job offer to practice law at a New York City firm upon graduation, but figured I would be up to the task as a player agent. Their reasoning was based on my legal education only in part. It was more for the trust we had built, the competitive spirit I had displayed on the court and the integrity that manifested itself during our post-game banter. They convinced me. I applied for my NFLPA certification during my third year of law school and moved to NYC shortly after graduation.

My first negotiation was with Deveron Harper. He was an undrafted free agent. I had all the information at my fingertips and my heart was beating quickly. He was a priority free agent, so my phone was ringing off the hook. The teams wanted a commitment right away. Time was of the essence, and I had to pick the right opportunity for him to make a team. We went back and forth on the signing bonus—which, admittedly, wasn't huge because he was an undrafted free agent. But those offers were barometers of how likely the team was to give him a real opportunity. I left the negotiation with Carolina confident that they expected him to really come in and compete for a roster spot. Afterward, I was spent. I felt like Rocky Balboa after he fought Apollo Creed—he had gone the distance but had to be put up in a hospital for the next two weeks.

As it turned out, my intuition about Deveron was correct. He made the 53-man roster and logged four NFL seasons.

I spent my first four years in NYC practicing intellectual property and transactional law with two top firms while representing only Notre Dame players on the side. The grind was unreal and exhausting, but that was why I absolutely loved it. I typically worked a 10-hour day at the firm before heading home. After making a quick meal or ordering delivery, I spent the next few hours working on agency-related matters—calling prospective Notre Dame clients, reviewing contracts and deals for current NFL clients, researching endorsement opportunities and media placements and brainstorming ways to add value to their careers both on and off the field. Bedtime was normally around 1:00am and I would be back at it at 6:00am to head to the gym for my morning workout before heading to the office and beginning the cycle all over again.

After four years of living this extreme, workaholic lifestyle, I began to realize two important things. First, I had an aptitude for the work I was performing on behalf of my NFL clients. Like the building of a perfect storm, the skill set and experience I was gaining as an associate in my law practice was sharpening, enhancing and refining my skills in contract review and negotiation on behalf of my NFL clients. My legal skill set flowed hand in hand with the work I was doing for these NFL players and allowed me to *excel*—to offer a service that I knew was going to be, if not the best, way at the top of what they were going to see in the industry at that time. Second, and more important, I realized that I absolutely loved the work. Working with young men of character from my alma mater to help them achieve a lifelong dream, provide for their families, make a difference in their communities and use their platform as a professional football player to enrich and uplift the lives of many. This *resonated* within me. It was the deep sense of fulfillment and satisfaction that got me out of bed every morning—no matter how tired I was—anxious and excited to tackle that day's work on behalf of my NFL clients.

So, after some extensive soul searching and prayer, I came to the epiphany that this was what I was born to do, to make a positive impact in the lives of these young men, to guide, protect and shepherd them in their professional careers, to inspire and advise them with integrity and faith to use their platform to make a difference, to witness to them and watch their backs at all times, to be *my brother's keeper*. I was armed only with a dream and an armor of faith, but I left the security of my firm, and launched my own agency. My dream had just begun.

Chapter 3

....

Playing the Game

"He who is not courageous enough to take risks will
accomplish nothing in life."
~ *Muhammad Ali*

For the first time in my life I didn't have the set, predetermined schedule of a commute to a classroom or an office. I didn't have a boss keeping me accountable. I had a computer, a phone, and the responsibility of a new agency on my shoulders. I would sink or swim on my own. There was suddenly no water cooler conversation and no staff meetings. The silence, in those moments, can be terrifying, but also exhilarating; knowing that I was building my agency according to my own blueprint and that I would answer to no one but myself.

Having burned the ships (as the ancient Spaniards did when conquering new lands to signify that there was no turning back), I attacked my new venture with a strategic action plan in place. While playing pickup games in high school, as the 1 (or point guard), I would full-court press the opposing team's point guard after *every* basket. I had the mindset that I was going to impose my will on the opposing player and wear him down through a battle of attrition—either into making mistakes or giving up the ball immediately upon receipt. It required a high-level of conditioning, commitment and mental toughness to press the entire game, but over time, I became respected for my will to win and became the hard-nosed, tenacious SOB that nobody wanted to play against. I took the same approach to my budding career as an NFL agent. I would press full-court for the entire game and earn the respect of my clients and peers through hard work, single-minded focus, creative vision, dynamic communication and integrity. I would leave every ounce of energy I had on the court in the pursuit of victory for my clients.

In building my agency, I knew that it was paramount to build it on a solid foundation of high-character clients. Like building a home on bedrock, I believed that an agency comprised of highly talented, high-character clients across the board would be able to withstand the inevitable storms of the player representation industry. Instead of spending invaluable time on ineffective matters such as bailing a client out of jail or preparing for a substance abuse appeal hearing, I would be able to allocate my time to more productive pursuits—like engaging Fortune 500 companies for endorsement deals, pitching national media outlets for client feature stories and preparing clients for their team interviews at the NFL Scouting Combine. Given our human nature, it is always easier to work your tail off for a client in whom you believe—not only as a player, but as a person as well. Players who appreciate the privilege of playing this great game for a living and who understand their obligation to pay it forward to the next generation. Ultimately, I knew that representing young men of character would pave my way to success in this field.

As I embarked on this journey, there were definitely some memorable bumps and potholes I encountered along the way. While I was home for spring break in March 1998 (and having been recently certified by the NFLPA), I attended the University of Akron Pro Day to support a local player and friend. It was a cold, rainy day so instead of running the forty on the artificial turf outdoors, it was held indoors on the hardwood basketball court. The participants at that pro day included my friend, former University of Akron wide receiver Devon Scott, and a fireplug of a linebacker from John Carroll University in whom the scouts seemed very interested, which was very surprising because the linebacker was no taller than me. In retrospect, I shouldn't have been so quick to dismiss this player. The undersized linebacker turned out to be London Fletcher, perennial All-Pro linebacker for the St. Louis Rams, Buffalo Bills and Washington Redskins.

Before the advent of the Internet, it was much more difficult for people to access photos and headshots in order to prepare for initial meetings. Such was the case in December 1999 when I flew one of my first clients, Deveron Harper, a cornerback for Notre Dame, out for a recruiting visit to NYC. Deveron and I had spoken over the phone several times and had developed a solid rapport so the trip was a natural segue in the agent vetting / client signing process. I took a taxi over to LaGuardia and made my way through security to meet and greet Deveron at the gate. As soon as Deveron got off the plane, I had a big smile on my face, hand out, ready to shake his hand. To my dismay, Deveron walked right by me as if I wasn't even there. As he continued to walk, I realized that he was not joking around. I yelled out to him "Deveron! Hey, Deveron!" Deveron turned around abruptly and centered his gaze on me. "Eugene Lee. Nice to finally meet you."

There was an unforgettable look on his face—like a nuanced combination of surprise and apprehension—before it quickly melted away and he smiled and shook my hand. The recruiting trip went extremely well and included Deveron's first experience with sushi (he loved it), seats to the Hornets vs. Knicks at Madison Square Garden and dinner at Michael Jordan's Steakhouse. It was during dinner that Deveron finally revealed to me the reason why he didn't recognize me when he got off the plane. "From our conversations on the phone, man, I didn't know you were Asian. I thought you were black!" We both broke up in hysterical laughter. After the laughter had subsided, I came to two important conclusions. One, apparently, I sounded like Barry White on the phone. Two, I realized that I had the goods to overcome a player's initial misconception by the stellar quality of my work and the dynamic, yet authentic, nature of our interaction, by making Deveron feel 100% confident and comfortable that I would do the absolute best job for him regardless of my race or the color of my skin. Well, after that initial case of mistaken identity, Deveron ended up signing with me and would go on to a 4-year career in the NFL.

Coincidentally, race played a part in another memorable experience with another Notre Dame player only a few weeks later. I flew to South Bend that January to meet with inside linebacker Ronnie Nicks. Ronnie was a compact, hydraulic coil of a linebacker who delivered devastating hits for the Fighting Irish that fall. He was fast, strong and explosive. It would've been a great signing for me so I prepared painstakingly for our meeting. Ronnie and I met up at LaSalle Grill and took our meeting upstairs to the jazz lounge after dinner. It was there that I finally got into my groove. I exuded confidence, expertise and passion for my work.

"Ronnie, no one will work harder, or more creatively, for you," I explained, really bringing the fire and brimstone. His dark eyes followed me, as he hung on my every word, mesmerized and captivated by my dynamic presentation, or so I thought.

After I had finished, Ronnie remained speechless before finally gathering himself to speak.

"Man, you look just like Bruce Lee."

I couldn't help, but laugh. Truth be told, I did have a little Enter the Dragon style going on at that time so Ronnie's comment wasn't totally out of left field. But, it did serve as a splash of cold water in the face—a humble reminder that as compelling of a presentation as I felt I delivered, it may have fallen on deaf ears due to an uninformed stereotype. The experience strengthened my resolve and reinforced in me the understanding that I would need to work harder, smarter and more creatively than ever before to overcome initial perceptions and make my mark in this industry.

My first order of business was building relationships in, around and throughout the NFL. I was fortunate to understand—even at a relatively young age—the incomparable importance of cultivating and leveraging relationships with decision makers for all 32 NFL teams in order to market my clients to the fullest and gain helpful information during the player evaluation process. So, I went to work. I took advantage of every opportunity I had to network, introduce myself and press the flesh with NFL scouts, personnel directors, coaches and GMs.

It was intimidating. I remember walking into the Crowne Plaza for the first time, seeing the autograph hounds swirling, and the scouts and GM's, all shuffling around in their team-logoed swag with a look on their faces that said, "Talk to me at your own peril." The athletes walked the lobby like kings in their free gear. It was a snowy, windy night in Indianapolis, which is typical for February. Having only a grainy Internet headshot as reference, I walked up to introduce myself to Jerry Angelo, GM of the Chicago Bears. He was as warm and friendly as he could possibly be. This meeting would be the start of a long, lasting friendship.

Jerry Jones is the only owner in the NFL who has a full-sized luxury party bus that travels wherever the team goes….including Indianapolis. I was out doing some networking on a Saturday night at the Combine and ended up on the Dallas Cowboys party bus back to the Marriott. It was an unforgettable experience meeting Stephen Jones (Jerry's son) and Larry Lacewell, this old, grizzled and legendary scout who had been in the league long before I was even born (and who gave me a good-natured ribbing for my "city" attire). It was a trip, in both the literal and figurative sense.

Whether it was at the Combine, Notre Dame Pro Day or East-West Shrine Game, I was respectful, yet confident, in my approach with the ultimate goal of building credibility, goodwill and trust with my NFL counterparts. Often, the best opportunities to network laid where you least expected them. A few years ago, I flew out to Notre Dame for the pro day to see Mike Richardson, a rising cornerback who could play stifling press coverage, but who also had the courage, aggressiveness and attitude to willingly come up and support the run. Mike also had the best nickname of any client I've ever repped. Apparently, Mike always looked older than his actual age, so when he was a freshman, Derek Curry, a junior linebacker, gave him the nickname "Uncle Mike." The nickname stuck for Mike's entire Notre Dame career and became an endearing term for his teammates.

Mike was a Combine snub so the Notre Dame Pro Day was his only opportunity to showcase his talent to NFL teams. I was looking forward to the opportunity to follow up his workout (we expected him to put up some very impressive numbers—which he did) by passing out additional information and game film to NFL teams in attendance. Unfortunately, my connecting flight to South Bend was delayed by several hours due to a delay on an inbound aircraft that had our flight crew. As I waited at the gate in Detroit, I began looking around and taking in my environment.

The Detroit airport is like the world's largest bus station. The old terminals were dirty and poorly lit. But as I sat at my gate—bummed about potentially missing the event—I looked around and saw the telltale NFL gear and tired faces of road-weary NFL scouts. I saw the team-logoed pullovers. They couldn't go anywhere either.

Silas McKinnie was there from the Detroit Lions. Andy Dengler was there from the Jacksonville Jaguars. I looked at this as an opportunity to make the most of my circumstances; to take lemons and make lemonade.

I took a deep breath and approached one of the scouts. "Silas, Eugene Lee of ETL Associates. I represent Mike Richardson from Notre Dame. I just wanted you to know that he is prepared and ready to test through the roof tomorrow. Do you have any questions for me, or any particular game film you'd like to see?"

I used the flight delay to network, market and push Mike, and to prep everyone for the outstanding pro day performance that was about to come. All 32 NFL teams had good grades on Mike because of what the game film had shown. There is a time-tested NFL adage that says, "the eye in the sky does not lie," and that is an absolute truth in the NFL world. Using Mike's stellar tape as validation to legitimize their time and mine, I then hammered home the point that Mike would *run well*. In fact, I felt so sure of Mike's forty time that I had made a friendly bet a couple of weeks earlier with my good friend Jerry Angelo, General Manager of the Chicago Bears. Jerry liked Mike a lot, but had questions about his overall speed. Jerry stated his case ("Eugene, Mike Richardson is a good football player and we like him a lot, but he is not a sub 4.5 guy"), but I knew better (having watched Mike train for the previous few weeks) and thus a friendly wager was born— whether or not Mike Richardson would run under a 4.5 at the Notre Dame Pro Day. I won the bet. Mike posted a time of 4.48 in the forty and also set an unofficial record of 6.27 seconds in the 3 cone drill (a drill which measures lateral quickness and agility).

In speaking with Jerry a couple months later, I found out that another reason he liked his odds was because of the notoriously slow watch of Chicago Bears Midwest scout Jeff Shiver. Apparently, even if a player times a 4.45 on most watches, he'll come in at 4.53 or somewhere in that neighborhood on Shiver's watch. Despite the long odds, I still emerged victorious as did Mike. He was drafted in the sixth round by the New England Patriots. He came out of training camp that year with a new nickname, "Moss Killer," because he was locking up Randy Moss every day in practice and having a phenomenal camp. Mike was having such a great camp that he ended up starting the third preseason game at nickelback against the Carolina Panthers (ahead of first-round defensive back Brandon Meriweather).

I was at a sports bar in New York City, on cloud nine, watching the game with my wife and a good friend. It felt so rewarding to see a client playing a significant role on the field.

Unfortunately, on a freak play while making a tackle in the first half, Mike broke his finger and wrist and was put on IR the next day. The injury may have shortened his career (although Mike went on to play three more seasons in the NFL), but he lived and achieved his dream.

Over time, I learned to develop relationships even in the most difficult situations. Despite a strong pre-season and having just switched to wide receiver the year before, my client and former Notre Dame quarterback Carlyle Holiday was released by the Arizona Cardinals after their final pre-season game. Although Carlyle did not make the final 53 man roster, the Cardinals did express interest in signing him to their practice squad. This was still quite an accomplishment for a former college quarterback with one-year of experience at wide receiver under his belt. John Idzik, Director of Football Administration, called me to review and discuss the terms of Carlyle's practice squad contract. I don't know if it was my meticulous attention to detail, straightforward communication style or simply my genuine concern for Carlyle's well-being, but John gained respect for the work I was doing on behalf of my client and we struck up a friendship which has lasted for the last ten years. Our friendship has endured his move to the Seattle Seahawks as their Vice President of Football Operations, and ultimately, to NYC where he became general manager of the New York Jets in 2013. John's tenure in New York ended more abruptly than we all had hoped, but that should not detract from his professional acumen and steadfast integrity.

The Combine has always afforded me a tremendous opportunity to press the flesh and build relationships with NFL personnel. Where else in the world can you have scouts, coaches, personnel directors and GMs for all 32 NFL teams located within a one-mile radius with the frigid temperatures and biting winter wind mitigated by downtown Indianapolis' intricate system of indoor walkways? It was at the Combine that I first met and became friends with Eliot Wolf, Director of Player Personnel for the Green Bay Packers. Eliot is the son of Hall of Fame NFL executive Ron Wolf who engineered Super Bowl champion teams for the Oakland Raiders and Green Bay Packers in his heralded NFL career. As the son of an NFL personnel executive, Eliot grew up timing forties at the Combine ever since he was ten-years old. Eliot has a brilliant football mind and is well on his way to earning a GM role with an NFL team in the very near future. A few years ago, I had asked Eliot to provide me with a testimonial quote to insert in our marketing materials. Eliot said he would be more than happy to oblige. True to his word, he emailed me his testimonial in the late morning. Before I could even send the testimonial to our graphic designer, I received a phone call from Eliot that same afternoon. Eliot informed me that the Packers were cutting my client Lorne Sam, a wide receiver/tight end hybrid from UTEP who had gone to camp with the Denver Broncos the year before because they needed his roster spot to address an injury at another position. After receiving the call, I took a moment to digest what had just transpired. It was the perfect illustration of the symbiotic, yet adversarial, relationship between agents and NFL teams. A poignant example of the love and hate, give-and-take dynamic that runs quietly behind the scenes to fuel the well-oiled NFL machine. In order to fully service your clients, you must develop friendships with NFL personnel at all levels; *however*, you must keep in mind that the NFL is a cutthroat business and there will always be an inherently adversarial relationship between an NFL team and a player's agent—even if your NFL front office friend gives you a heartfelt testimonial.

Hardened a bit by that perspective, I had my guard up during my initial conversations with Jerry Angelo, former general manager of the Chicago Bears. Jerry first contacted me several years ago, regarding a client of mine from Ohio State, Tyler Everett, a free safety from my hometown of Canton, OH. The Bears had strong interest in Tyler that year so Jerry and I kept in contact frequently in the months leading up to the NFL Draft. It was through these conversations that a genuine, lasting friendship was born. Jerry and I had several things in common—from growing up in Northeastern Ohio (Jerry was from Youngstown, 45 minutes east of Canton), to love of Notre Dame and fondness for good Italian food and red wine—and as our friendship developed, I appreciated and absorbed the brilliant snippets of scouting wisdom that he used to impart on a regular basis. Snippets such as "NFL teams will always grade to a player's ceiling" (meaning that NFL teams will view game film on a player, note the highest potential that he exhibits on tape and extrapolate that level of play on a consistent basis once he gets to the next level—this is why teams will always take projection over production at the collegiate level), "Look for a player with special traits" (meaning that you want to find a player who exhibits special qualities—whether they be athletic, character or a combination of both) and "The farther away you get from the center of the field, the more special you need to be athletically" (which makes perfect sense when you take into consideration that cornerbacks and wide receivers are the fastest, most athletic guys on a football team). Jerry was under no obligation to impart his wisdom to me, a young agent in the business who could only offer little in return, but he must've seen something in me to which he could relate, whether it was the hunger to compete and win, the drive to put in countless hours to pursue greatness or the integrity and faith that served as the foundation for my professional pursuits and personal life. Jerry Angelo is a true gentleman and class act in every sense of the word. He became, and still is, a dear friend, whom I respect and admire for his unparalleled knowledge of the game of football and business of the NFL, but more important, for his kindness and boundless generosity in taking a young agent under his wing many years ago.

I live by the motto that you reap what you sow, and over the years, my diligent efforts to build my network of NFL contacts has placed me in the favorable position I am in today. When I started in the industry, I cultivated friendships with scouts and player personnel assistants for all 32 NFL teams. Over the years, as we've risen through the ranks together, the guys of my generation have ascended to top-level GM positions throughout the NFL. GMs such as Ryan Grigson (Colts), John Schneider (Seahawks), Reggie McKenzie (Raiders), John Dorsey (Chiefs), Ray Farmer (Browns), Thomas Dimitroff (Falcons) and Les Snead (Rams). I like to say my generation is in power. These men are at the highest levels of decision-making power across the NFL, yet I can still approach them based on the friendships we've built over the years to market and service my clients to the fullest. I can rely on my credibility and reputation to ensure that much of the information placed before them will be truly evaluated, analyzed, read and given consideration. My clients benefit directly from this goodwill, which is the grease that ends up oiling the vehicle to their future NFL careers.

Once a team has made its decision and drafted my client, the real fun begins. When I meet with a prospective client and his family, I let them know that contract negotiation is my Super Bowl. It is the Lombardi Trophy for which I strive, prepare, sacrifice and toil for hours upon end. It is the perfect convergence of my educational background, legal training, experience and dynamic communication skills to achieve two very important goals for my clients: (1) maximize guaranteed money; and (2) negotiate precise contractual language to protect that guaranteed money over the entire contract term.

Several years ago, I represented arguably the #1 fullback in the draft, Deon Anderson, out of the University of Connecticut. Deon was drafted in the 6th Round by the Dallas Cowboys (more on that to come) and as training camp approached that July, I began contract negotiations with Todd Williams of the Dallas Cowboys. I enjoyed negotiating with Todd. He was a sharp, yet laid back, guy who definitely stayed true to his country roots (I couldn't help, but smile every time I heard Johnny Cash's "Ring of Fire" on his cell). Negotiations went along relatively smoothly and we finally came to an agreement on Deon's signing bonus a few days before training camp was about to begin. When Todd sent over the paperwork to finalize the contract, my first move was to review the signing bonus default addendum. A signing bonus default addendum is included as part of every NFL team's standard player contract. It grants an NFL team the right to demand repayment of all, or a portion of, a player's signing bonus for conduct detrimental to the team (which could include felony convictions, multiple drug offenses and a voluntary refusal or failure to practice or play). Signing bonus default addenda began popping up across the NFL in the late 1990s as signing bonuses began to escalate and risky off-the-field behavior by players such as Rae Carruth (convicted for conspiracy to commit murder) and Bam Morris (drug trafficking) prompted teams to search for some type of mechanism to protect their long-term investments.

As I reviewed the Cowboys signing bonus default language, one particular phrase jumped out at me. The questionable language required Deon to repay a portion of his signing bonus (based on a four-year default repayment schedule) for "incarceration or conviction of a felony offense." I took a long, hard look at that language and it finally dawned on me. Under the US judicial system, there is a presumption of innocence in any criminal case. You are deemed innocent until proven guilty—until your guilt is proven beyond a reasonable doubt. I then thought about high-profile sports figures—including future Hall of Famers Ray Lewis and Kobe Bryant—who were incarcerated for felony offenses and later exonerated and found *not guilty* in a court of law. Under this exact language, if the same circumstances were to hold true for my client, the Cowboys would technically be within their rights to go after Deon's signing bonus. Now, 99% of the time, this addendum would not even be applicable to the types of clients I represent, however, my job was (and is) to protect my players' guaranteed money over the short and long-term under any and all possible circumstances and scenarios. So, I called Todd and told him that I would need the word "incarceration" to be stricken in order for us to sign.

Todd balked. "Eugene, Tony Romo has this language in his contract, T.O. has this language in his!" I countered, "Todd, with all due respect, I am not representing Tony Romo or Terrell Owens. I am representing Deon Anderson and until I am 100% comfortable with this default language and the security of my client's signing bonus, I am advising my client not to sign."

A couple days passed and training camp drew even closer.

Training camp is a team's built-in bargaining lever, as they know athletes grow more paranoid by the day as training camp—and real competition—nears. They don't want to miss one rep that could potentially go to another player competing for their spot. Finally, Todd called. It turns out, Todd had done some research and discovered that from the time Jerry Jones had bought the Dallas Cowboys in 1990, the Cowboys had never gone after a single player's signing bonus under their default addendum. This was even more compelling when taken in the context of Duane Goodrich's felony conviction for vehicular homicide in 2001. Goodrich had been a defensive back for the Cowboys at the time of the crime. Even then, the Cowboys had not gone after his signing bonus. This unspoken organizational doctrine was extremely important because it established course of dealing. Course of dealing is a pattern of consistent behavior over a long period of time which precludes an individual or entity from acting in a totally inconsistent manner when there has been reliance on such long-time behavior. Under this legal theory, the Cowboys would've had a difficult time asserting their right to repayment of Deon's signing bonus if he were ever incarcerated. Fully satisfied that my client's signing bonus would be secured irrespective of the default language, I advised Deon to sign. Deon would go on to a four-year NFL career with the Dallas Cowboys and Miami Dolphins.

A couple years later, my agency had the good fortune of representing another top fullback, Tony Fiammetta, out of Syracuse. Tony was drafted in the 4th Round by the Carolina Panthers as the first fullback chosen that year. During contract negotiations, in an effort to maximize the upfront signing bonus, I opted for a four-year contract term with a base salary escalator in Year Four. A base salary escalator is a contractual mechanism that can escalate (or more than double) your client's base salary in Year Four provided that certain playtime (percentage of offensive or defensive snaps) and team statistical ranking requirements are met in Years One to Three.

I understood that as a true old school fullback in a pro-style offense, Tony would be subbed out on passing downs. I knew that for my client to even have a chance of hitting the base salary escalator, we would need to keep that playtime percentage requirement as low as possible. In my opinion, a playtime percentage requirement at, or under, 35% would allow Tony a realistic chance to hit this escalator. We emerged victorious. The playtime percentage was set at 35%. The overall significance of what I had negotiated did not dawn on me until the following year when John Conner (the #1 fullback in the draft taken in the 5th Round by the New York Jets) agreed to terms on a four-year contract with a base salary escalator and a 50% playtime percentage requirement.

In addition to examining the big picture and thinking through every possible outcome for your client, the basic, yet often overlooked, secret to successful contract negotiation is to be overly meticulous and thorough in your review. I make it a point to always double and even triple check my work to ensure that all the i's are dotted and the t's are crossed—because you can never forget the adversarial nature of an NFL team's relationship with your client ... and what that often entails.

During my negotiation of a proposed injury settlement with the New York Giants for my long-time client Brian Witherspoon, I had expected to see language specifying his left anterior cruciate ligament, which he had torn twice in back-to-back seasons. I did see that language, but to my surprise, I also saw language in the release pertaining to "trauma to the body generally." The insertion of this clause was a shrewd attempt by the Giants to protect their organization from any future claims that Brian would have for any injuries totally unrelated to his knee. The broad language would cover any type of injury to any other body part. Needless to say, I asked the Giants to strike this clause before taking our negotiations any further on the monetary aspect of the settlement.

"Matt, this is Eugene Lee, I had an opportunity to review the settlement you sent me, but the clause at the end makes no sense at all. There's no way my client will sign this settlement with that clause at the end. The settlement needs to be very specific to the injury he sustained. You'll need to strike that clause completely if you want us to sign it."

They knew what they were doing, and I didn't get much pushback from Matt. Within 24 hours, I received a new copy of the agreement with the offending clause removed.

Ambiguous language reared its ugly head again with the Kansas City Chiefs. The Chiefs wanted to sign my client Mike Richardson after he had been released by the Patriots, but required a waiver for a preexisting injury to his shoulder which would've protected them in the event that Mike were to hurt the same shoulder again. With a signed injury waiver in place, the Chiefs would've been able to release Mike without placing him on Injured Reserve, where he would've continued to receive his base salary for the remainder of the season. In a perfect world, we would've never agreed to the waiver, however, the Chiefs were our only suitor at the time and had a need at cornerback so we both felt that the waiver was a necessary evil to Mike's next opportunity in the league. When I received the injury waiver from the Chiefs, I immediately noticed that they had the wrong shoulder listed. That was strike one. Strike two was the overly broad description of the preexisting injury. The wording was way too general. When an injury waiver is negotiated for your client, you want the language to be as scientifically precise as possible in order to fully protect your client. Instead of exposing your client to the risk that any future shoulder injury would fall under the broad umbrella of "injury to left shoulder" and disqualify him from being compensated under his collectively bargained rights, the preferred approach would be to meticulously describe the preexisting injury as, "subluxation of the fourth capsule at the insertion of the humerus." (Having a brother for a medical doctor did provide me with an unfair advantage in this negotiation).

The Chiefs were probably wondering where I came up with my surprisingly in-depth knowledge of the human anatomy, but they eventually conceded and accepted my proposed language, and Mike went on to play out the rest of the season, without injury, I might add.

Although a good agent is defined by his work in contract negotiation, an even better one utilizes all information available at his fingertips to place his client in the best possible position to succeed. There is an art to leveraging legitimate team interest to maximize and even elevate your client's draft status. If done tactfully and strategically, you and your client can reap the rewards for years to come. There is no better time to employ these tactics than during the NFL Draft.

Ever since my first client, I have charted the entire NFL Draft. The reason for doing so is twofold. One, you can monitor which teams selected players at your client's position (and in which rounds) so you can place your client in the best possible position to make a team should he need to go the undrafted free agent route. Two, by keeping tabs on players selected at your client's position, you can begin to strategically maneuver and leverage another team(s) interest to force a team's hand and select your player earlier than they would have—if at all—in the later rounds of the draft.

Going into the 2007 NFL Draft, I knew that there were a handful of teams that had high grades on Deon Anderson, as the #1 fullback on their board including the Dallas Cowboys, the only team to bring Deon in for an official pre-draft visit after the Combine. Just as NFL teams have their draft "war rooms," we had a room set up in the conference area of our ETL offices. Manned with phones, notepads, and numbers for every NFL team, we hustled and worked the phones just like the teams. Our hopes rose and fell with every name that came off the board. We watched ESPN and the NFL Network just like fans at home, and just like teams across the country. There is no better human drama.

As the draft played out that year, only one fullback, LeRon McClain from Alabama, had been selected heading into the sixth round. As the picks flashed by in Round Six, I received a phone call from Anthony Lynn, newly hired running backs coach for the Cleveland Browns. Ironically enough, Coach Lynn had just come from the Cowboys where he had interviewed and evaluated Deon at the Combine. The purpose of the call was to express Cleveland's interest in signing Deon as a priority free agent if he was not drafted. As soon as the call ended, I took a quick look at the draft order for the remaining picks in the sixth round. The Cowboys had the 200th pick and the Browns were sitting five spots ahead of them with the 195th pick.

With Cleveland's pick fast approaching; I knew I only had a small window of opportunity, so I seized it. I picked up the phone and made a quick call to Chris Hall, College Scouting Coordinator for the Cowboys. I told Chris that Anthony Lynn had just called and that the Browns had expressed strong interest in Deon. What really played into our favor was Coach Lynn's familiarity with Deon from his stint in Dallas. The natural assumption would've been that he would be giving his own personal scouting report on Deon to his new employer. As Chris vigorously pressed me for further details, I told him that was all that was conveyed to me. I figured I would let Dallas figure out the rest—which they did. Shortly after the Browns were on the clock, I saw a "TRADE" announcement pop up on the screen. Dallas had just traded its sixth round pick (#200) and its seventh round pick (#234) to Cleveland for their sixth round pick (#195). I anxiously waited for what was to come next.

After what seemed like an eternity, Dallas finally submitted its pick. "DEON ANDERSON—FULLBACK, UCONN" flashed across the screen and our draft room erupted in euphoric celebration! Trades typically do not happen that late in the draft (in fact, Dallas' trade to Cleveland was the final trade in the 2007 NFL Draft), but I was able to capitalize on the information at hand to provide my client with the best opportunity to embark on his NFL career.

I employed a similar strategy behind the scenes (which was captured for posterity on ESPN's "The Dotted Line") in my work for Jacquian Williams during the 2011 NFL Draft. After watching outside linebacker after outside linebacker come off the board, I entered the sixth round of the draft with a sense of urgency. I made it my mission to utilize all available information at my disposal in order to up the ante. After his spectacular pro day performance, Jacquian had taken five official pre-draft visits with NFL teams. While examining the draft order in the sixth round, I began to text GMs, scouts and personnel directors for these teams in advance of their picks to alert them of the fact that another team that had also brought Jacquian in for a visit was due to pick a few spots behind them. My goal was to spur one of these teams to pull the trigger and draft Jacquian rather than risk losing him to another team a few picks behind.

With the Chicago Bears (one of Jacquian's pre-draft visit teams) having selected West Virginia outside linebacker J. T. Thomas at Pick #195, I centered my sights on the New York Giants (another one of Jacquian's pre-draft visit teams) sitting at Pick #202. I texted Giants assistant general manager Kevin Abrams to give him the heads up that the Seattle Seahawks—sitting three picks behind at Pick #205—had also brought Jacquian in for a pre-draft visit and had called me a few days before the draft to reaffirm their interest in taking an outside linebacker in the later rounds. As I stated in the documentary, Kevin's "typical noncommittal response" shed no greater light on the Giants plans, but my work was done. After a few tense moments, our draft room exploded into jubilant celebration as "JACQUIAN WILLIAMS—LINEBACKER, SOUTH FLORIDA" flashed across the screen.

Just because the draft has ended, it does not mean my work is done. I have a responsibility to market my undrafted clients to the right NFL teams as tenaciously and strategically as possible. Through trial and error, I've learned the subtle importance of contacting the person in charge of "fielding" the team (and not the field itself).

Immediately after the 2008 NFL Draft, I was trying to place a client of mine as an undrafted free agent. The player was a defensive back for the University of Michigan and the Patriots Midwest scout at the time, Jim Nagy, was also a UM grad who loved Michigan players. Jim had a fourth round grade on my client entering the draft, so I figured the Patriots would be a natural first choice for us. Scott Pioli, former general manager of the Kansas City Chiefs, was running the player personnel department for the Patriots at the time. Scott has become a good friend of mine over the years, but he had a reputation for being very gruff with agents, especially young agents whom he did not know that tried to solicit him about players via email. I did have Scott's email address though and, like most NFL teams, the Patriots followed a particular format which was first name + first initial of last name@patriots.com. So, I'm thinking to myself, okay, I can put two and two together—Jim Nagy's email address would be jimn@patriots.com. Having figured out Jim's email address, I proceeded to send this very pointed email describing my client's best games, workout results and high character traits. I reassured Jim that given the opportunity my client would come in to camp, compete his tail off and make the Patriots a better team. Feeling satisfied with the email I had drafted, I waited to hear some positive news. In hindsight, I should've texted Jim.

The next morning, I received an email back from a bewildered Scott Pioli asking me, "Eugene, why are you emailing our head groundskeeper about your client?" It turns out that the email address I had used was for Jim Nolan, the SVP of Stadium Operations for the Patriots! I never did figure out Jim Nagy's correct email address, however, Scott Pioli and I have forged a friendship that has endured.

I was one of the many who reached out to Scott with thoughts and prayers after the senseless Jovan Belcher tragedy a few years ago, and that meant a great deal to Scott. No one can ever understand why a young NFL player, in the prime of his career, would take the life of his girlfriend and then turn the gun on himself, leaving behind an orphaned infant daughter. It was a situation in which we were reminded of the real brokenness that exists in the world and in our own hearts. It was a reminder that behind the money and the dreams, life in the NFL is still hopelessly complicated and empty for many. It was a reminder that the NFL dream—as great as it is—is ultimately not trustworthy…it wasn't for Jovan Belcher, it wasn't for Scott, and it wasn't for me. The NFL is a good gift, but a bad idol.

In those moments, human connections and God's sovereignty are everything. I was reminded of not only the brevity of an NFL career…but of life itself.

Beyond the game of football, it's about compassion and love for your clients and brothers within the NFL fraternity. That is the eternal perspective that will fuel you to go above and beyond in building your agency with the right clientele—players in whom you believe, both on and off the field.

Chapter 4

The Road Warrior

"Let your plans be dark and impenetrable as night, and when you move, fall like a thunderbolt."

~ Sun Tzu

I parked my rental car and made my way up the elevator to the high-rise Chicago condo where I would meet Notre Dame running back Robert Hughes. Robert was a thick, explosive rock of a running back who was underutilized at Notre Dame, and may have even projected as a fullback at the next level.

The door opened and soon I was surrounded by concerned family members, parents, friends, and trainers—all part of a de jure and de facto "team" that is assembled by draft prospects. There is an uncertain excitement in these rooms. It's the excitement that comes from proximity to a world-class athlete and the potential that represents. However, it's the uncertainty that troubles the people in this room...whose dreams rest on the powerful, sloping shoulders of Robert Hughes.

I had just finished the book "Unbroken," by Laura

Hillenbrand. The book retold the inspirational real life story of Olympian and World War II hero Louie Zamperini, a true testament to the human spirit and power of perseverance. As I prepared for my meeting with Robert, I decided to incorporate the story of "Unbroken" into my presentation. Robert had persevered in his own right during his roller coaster Notre Dame career so I thought he would relate to the book's central theme.

"Robert, even though you had an amazing high school career and a great start at Notre Dame," I said, "You faced the adversity of sharing a backfield with Armando Allen. But like Louie Zamperini in the book … you persevered. You remained unbroken."

From that opening monologue, I launched into a high-energy presentation fueled by fire and brimstone. I described our detailed pre-draft strategy for overcoming Robert's limited playing time during his senior season to showcase his special traits to NFL teams, which were exceptionally quick feet for a man his size, extraordinary vision to see cutback lanes and the best hands out of the backfield in the draft. I ended my presentation by looking Robert in the eye and telling him we were kindred spirits, men who would never surrender, despite seemingly insurmountable odds, in pursuit of their dreams. As I peered around the room, every eye was transfixed on me as heads began to nod. I had connected on an emotional level with every person in that room, including Robert, who would go on and sign with me later that month. This is the buzz of sports-agenting. It is sincerity mixed with the thrill of performance.

There is a certain romantic appeal associated with the athlete representation industry, which has undoubtedly been reinforced by the Hollywood glamorization of films such as

Jerry Maguire. However, the reality of this business is that you must be willing to sacrifice, to spend countless hours on the road, to live out of a suitcase, to endure sleep deprivation and, in certain situations, even place yourself in harm's way to make your mark and succeed. You must absolutely love the work because if you don't, you will quickly find yourself on the side of the road catching the next bus out of town. You must be willing to work harder, more strategically and more tenaciously than the competition—at all times.

Nowhere is this mindset more prevalent than in the ultra-competitive, cutthroat world of player recruitment. When I meet with a player, I go in with supreme confidence, understanding and believing with every ounce of energy in my heart and soul that there is no other decision for this young man to make, but to sign with me. There are no other agents. There is only him and me. That type of confidence, if fully believed from the depths of your soul, will come across to a young man and his family. There's a gleam in my eye when I discuss my competitive advantage, what makes my representation unique and how it will make a difference in a player's career, both in the short and long-term. I don't discuss other agencies or agents. I have never felt the need to elevate myself by talking negatively about other agents. I have always accentuated and emphasized the positive in my presentations because I believe a victory is that much sweeter when earned on its merits. In the manic world of college football recruiting, it's hard sometimes for a young man to tune out the white noise to get to the symphony, but you just keep on playing your song.

The following year, I recruited Florida running back Jeff Demps. He was a football player who happened to run track. He was shifty in and out of his breaks, and he had excellent hands out of the backfield. Honestly, I had never seen speed like his on a college football field. He routinely outran the pursuit angles of college defensive backs. It was impressive.

More important, through a close NFL scouting contact, I found out he was a really good kid and a man of high character. I knew he'd be a fit for us. I was able to leverage a contact with an NFL scout, who put me in touch with Jeff. I set up a visit with him after the Vanderbilt game that fall. It was a recruiting coup for me because I had always wanted to break into the SEC and establish myself at a program like Florida's.

I met with him at his apartment the morning after the game. My creative team had created a great three-minute highlight video. Unfortunately I was subject to the whims of the 3G connection I had, so there was a lot of pressing "play" and "stop." But Jeff was a good sport about it. He was arguably the fastest player in college football and qualified for the US Olympic Trials in the 100m. As I prepared for our meeting, I decided to incorporate the theme of speed into my presentation, since it was his defining trait. As I sat with Jeff, I emphasized to him that my work as an agent would be akin to his game-breaking ability on the field. That to run ahead of the pack takes skill, speed, conviction and courage which was similar to my style of player representation, where I was continually looking for ways to run ahead of the pack and break new ground. Although Jeff eventually decided to forego the NFL Draft in favor of training for the 2012 Summer Olympics (rumors were that the Florida coaching staff's decision to utilize Chris Rainey, a running back with a similar skill set, more extensively than Jeff that fall may have prompted his decision to pursue track and field), I left that meeting convinced that we had found common ground in the universal language of speed.

I learned early on in the industry that a prerequisite for success in recruiting is to be confident and comfortable in any environment. One of my first clients from Notre Dame, defensive end Lamont Bryant, played in the Blue-Gray Classic in Montgomery, AL. The historic all-star game has long since been discontinued, but it was played every year on Christmas Day from 1939-2001. That year, I flew down to Montgomery a couple days before Christmas to meet with Lamont. After my presentation, Lamont asked me if I had any plans that evening. I told him I did not have any set plans so Lamont invited me out with a bunch of players who were going to a nightclub called The Rose in downtown Montgomery. When we arrived at the club, we discovered a long line halfway down the block. Apparently, there was a rap concert that night and the club was packed to the gills. Fortunately, we were given the VIP treatment and allowed to sidestep the line. As we entered the club, I took a quick look around and noticed that I was the only non-African American person in the entire club.

After taking in the scene, I also came to the conclusion that I won the prize for most formally dressed as I was the only person in the club wearing a suit and tie. Despite standing out in my surroundings, I had never before felt so comfortable in any environment—even though it wasn't an environment where I would normally find myself. I felt at ease and confident as I began to navigate the club. After a while, I began to notice the stares of women who were trying to figure me out. They must have been thinking, "Man, this guy's got some swag in him to walk around here dressed in a suit and tie." It was an empowering feeling and it was at that moment that I fully understood the true definition of strength. There is strength in confidence, in being yourself, in standing out from the crowd and in carrying yourself with dignity and grace. There is unyielding strength in being fearless, tenacious and supremely confident in any environment. You can transcend stereotypes and affect people's opinions based upon your words, your actions and your integrity. Have the strength to allow your character to shine through so that people will judge you for who you are and not by the color of your skin or race.

I have taken this open-minded attitude with me to recruiting visits all over the United States. A few years ago, I met with a defensive back from Southern Mississippi who lived in a lower income area of New Orleans down by the levies. His home had one bedroom and although there were at least 6 or 7 younger siblings sitting on the couch in the living room watching television, the bedroom belonged solely to him because he was the big-time D1 athlete who represented the ticket out. I presented to him while I sat on the bed in his room. The setting for our meeting was unlike any I had ever been in before, but once I settled into my groove, all distractions faded and I was able to deliver my presentation with passion, poise and authenticity. Nonetheless, it was a jarring juxtaposition—the promise of future wealth mixed with the current reality of poverty.

Off an inside tip from Jerry Angelo, I recruited a quarterback from Eastern Michigan named Andy Schmitt in the fall of 2009. I had established a solid rapport with Andy over the summer and planned a trip to Ann Arbor during the second week of the season to watch him play against Big Ten competition in the form of the Michigan Wolverines. I navigated the tiny, labyrinthine streets of Ann Arbor around "The Big House," where I would be one of 100,000 in the stands.

After a solid first half, Andy dropped back to throw early

in the third quarter and crumbled to the turf clutching his right knee. It was a non-contact injury and I feared the worst. I still ended up meeting with Andy on crutches at his apartment after the game and although I could tell he was crestfallen, he tried his best to put on a good face saying that the MRI was scheduled for Monday and that there was not that much pain in the knee. One of the most difficult experiences I have ever had in recruiting was my meeting with Andy that fateful Saturday afternoon. We should have been celebrating the thrill of competing against a legendary program in front of a huge crowd…instead we were navigating the reality that for a fringe prospect from an under-the-radar program, this could be the end of his professional football hopes.

Although I tried my best to exude optimism and deliver my presentation with hope and enthusiasm, in the bottom of my heart, I knew that he had torn his ACL…and I felt awful. There was a hollow pit in my stomach the entire time because I understood the cruel reality he was about to face. Andy's football career ended that Saturday afternoon and A. E. Housman's poem ("To the Athlete Dying Young") never rang so true and poignantly as it did for me that day.

Effective recruiting requires a near maniacal level of commitment and sacrifice. Long days and even longer nights are a nonnegotiable part of the job description. One of my most epic recruiting trips took place several years ago with my good friend Dwayne Harper, former All-Pro cornerback for the Seattle Seahawks and San Diego Chargers, who was working with me at the time as my Director of Player Development. Dwayne and I flew in to Lexington, KY on a Saturday morning and rented a car to drive to Frankfurt, KY to watch Stillman College play Kentucky State. We spent some quality time with Stillman cornerback/kick returner Brian Witherspoon immediately after the game (which would turn out to be time well spent because Brian would go on to sign a month later) and then hopped on the road to drive six hours to South Bend, IN. Notre Dame had played Navy at home that afternoon and we had a breakfast meeting scheduled with Notre Dame linebacker Joe Brockington and an early afternoon meeting with the older brother of Notre Dame defensive end Trevor Laws on Sunday after the game. We arrived in South Bend around 10:30p.m. and headed to the hotel, physically and mentally exhausted from the events of the day. The meetings went well on Sunday, but as soon as our last one had ended, Dwayne and I were back on the road driving another five hours from South Bend to Cincinnati where we had booked departing flights to NYC and Columbia, SC. Luckily, there were no flight delays that evening.

A couple years ago, I had a meeting scheduled with the mother and uncle of former Virginia and current Washington Redskins lineman Morgan Moses in Richmond, VA. Using Washington, DC as a gauge (which is only 3.5 hours away from NYC by car), I decided to drive down to the meeting. It was only when I hopped into my car and looked at my GPS that I realized the distance from NYC to Richmond was much further than to DC (six hours to be exact). Luckily, our meeting was scheduled for 7:00p.m. that evening so I had ample time—or so I thought. Unfortunately, there were several accidents on I-95 that day and my six-hour drive took me nearly eight hours. I pulled into the parking lot of Firebird Restaurant a couple of minutes before 7:00p.m. Despite my harried arrival, the meeting went extraordinarily well and lasted for 2 hours and 45 minutes. I left Richmond at

10:30p.m. and although I had initially planned to stay overnight at a hotel near Washington, DC, my adrenaline was flowing and the music was pumping, so about two hours into my drive, I made up my mind to drive all the way back to NYC. When I arrived home at 4:45am that morning, I had spent more than 14 hours on the road that day sandwiched around a nearly three-hour meeting!

Long hours are not always confined to the road. During my recruitment of former Oregon tight end David Paulson, his final agent meetings were scheduled in Eugene, OR on a Saturday afternoon in mid-December. Due to a crazy workweek, I ended up taking a 6:00am flight out of JFK that Saturday morning which connected to Eugene through Salt Lake City. I arrived in Eugene around 1:00p.m. PST, headed to the hotel to wash up and prepare for my meeting and drove to the Ducks' facility. The meeting went well and lasted from 5:00p.m.—7:00p.m. PST. After the meeting, I grabbed a quick bite at an Outback Steakhouse and headed back to the hotel to catch some much needed ZZZs. I was up bright and early the next morning to catch a 6:00am flight out of Eugene to Salt Lake City where I connected on another flight back to JFK. I arrived back in NYC around 5:00p.m. that Sunday evening vowing to never take a 24-hour cross-country trip ever again. On another occasion, I was forced to burn the midnight oil before departing for the Michigan vs. Michigan State game to meet with star Spartan cornerback Darqueze Dennard. I was up till the wee hours of the morning tweaking a brand development deck we had prepared for Darqueze while sending last-minute edits to our video team for his highlight video. I fell asleep with my fingers crossed hoping that the A/V crew would be able to turn around final edits before my early morning departure. Luckily for me, they rose to the occasion. I woke up at 5:30a.m., downloaded Darqueze's highlight video to my iPad and hopped into a cab headed for LaGuardia. Armed with the tools of my trade, I left a lasting impression on Darqueze that weekend.

The best recruiting trips are the ones where you can kill two birds (or as many as you can) with one stone. I was recently able to incorporate a new client signing, prospective client meeting, current client dinner and breakfast with family in one 24 hour trip to Florida right before New Year's Eve. My flight arrived in Jacksonville around 11:00am and after grabbing a quick bite at the airport Chili's, I drove to meet Kecia Johnson, mother of Rutgers offensive lineman Kaleb Johnson, on her lunch break from work. We met at a barbeque place and had great first meeting. She talked to me about raising her boys as a single mother, and I gained a ton of respect for her. It was important for her to meet me, because I would be navigating her son through the turbulent waters of the "next level."

After our meeting, I then drove to the law office of Reginald Luster, a close family friend of the Johnsons, where I reviewed the NFLPA Standard Representation Agreement with Kaleb and Reginald before Kaleb signed the necessary paperwork to make our relationship official.

Feeling great about my new client, I departed Jacksonville at 4:00p.m. to drive to Tampa, approximately 230 miles away, where I had a meeting scheduled that evening with Corey Grant, a running back for Auburn who was in town for the Outback Bowl. While I was driving, it dawned on me that I had a client, Jeremiah Warren, offensive guard for the Tampa Bay Buccaneers, who lived very close to the Grand Hyatt (where the Auburn players were staying) so I texted Jeremiah and asked him to meet me at the hotel for a late dinner after my meeting with Corey. I ended up hitting heavy rush hour traffic in Orlando on I-4 and it began to rain heavily. Realizing that I was starving and would not have time to eat before my meeting with Corey, I exited I-4 to stop at a Wendy's drive-thru where I ordered a bowl of chili (yes, Wendy's chili is a staple of mine on the road). I ate my chili very carefully while driving to the Grand Hyatt and arrived around 9:30p.m. Upon my arrival, I texted Jeremiah to give him an updated ETA and scurried through the lobby to head up to Corey's room. As I was about to hop on the elevator, I decided at the very last second that it might be a good idea to make a quick pit stop in the lobby restroom to freshen up a bit before my meeting. It's a good thing I did.

As soon as I walked in and looked into the mirror, my jaw dropped in horror. Despite my best efforts, I had managed to splatter chili all over my sportcoat lapels! I couldn't help but laugh when I thought about what Corey's reaction would've been had I walked into our meeting with chili splattered all over myself. I would've looked like a sloppy clown! After gathering myself (and taking my sportcoat off, of course), I headed up to Corey's room where I presented for one hour. After our meeting, I met up with Jeremiah for a late night dinner in the lobby bar. Jeremiah and I caught up on some pending matters and I got back on the road at 11:10p.m. to drive back to Jacksonville. I pulled into the Omni that morning at 2:45a.m. and was up at 7:00a.m. the very next morning before hopping on my flight back to JFK. Needless to say, the beverage cart passed me by on the return flight.

However, these long days and nights all pale in comparison to the longest day of my life as a sports agent. Several years ago, I recruited a cornerback from the University of Missouri named Darnell Terrell. Darnell was from St. Louis and his father Cletus was a firefighter and a character. After my initial meeting with Cletus in St. Louis over the summer, Cletus invited Dwayne Harper and me to spend the day with him in St. Louis before driving up to Columbia to watch Darnell play against Nebraska that evening. I got up very early that Saturday morning to catch a 6:40a.m. flight to St. Louis and Dwayne's flight arrived around the same time. I rented a car and we left the airport around 10:00a.m. to meet Cletus for breakfast at a local pancake house. After our meal, we then accompanied Cletus to a Jiffy Lube so he could get the oil changed in his car. We left the gas station to head back to Cletus' house where we shot pool for an hour before accompanying him to a hand car wash in East St. Louis. As I waited in the lobby for Cletus' car to be washed, I couldn't help but notice the beautiful artwork on the walls. I gazed at the stunning, lifelike portraits of Louis Farrakhan, Elijah Muhammad, Malcolm X, Martin Luther King, Jr. and Maya Angelou and it was at that moment that I began to believe that Cletus was testing me. By taking me to a hand car wash in a predominantly black part of town, he wanted to know if I would be able to adapt and be comfortable in unfamiliar surroundings. I passed the test with flying colors (little did he know that I had already been to The Rose almost a decade before). Before leaving the carwash to hop on I-70, Cletus attached a furry tiger tail to the rear bumper of his car. We then drove two hours west to Columbia for the 8:00p.m. (CST) kickoff of Missouri vs. Nebraska.

After the game ended, Dwayne, Cletus and I drove to Darnell's apartment (sans furry tiger tail—to Cletus' disappointment, someone had stolen the tail off the back of his car) where we met with Darnell at 1:00a.m.—proof that you must always be ready to engage a potential client, no matter the time of day or night. Our presentation lasted for 90 minutes before we hopped back on the road to drive two hours back to St. Louis. I was sitting in the backseat of Cletus' car trying desperately to stay awake out of fear that he would fall asleep at the wheel. Thankfully, we made it back to Cletus' house in one piece and Dwayne and I said our good-byes and got into our rental car at 4:45a.m. to drive to our hotel.

I'll never forget Dwayne's comment on the ride over that "we better sign this kid after going through all this." We arrived at the hotel around 5:15am and Dwayne took a quick thirty minute catnap before leaving for his 7:00a.m. flight. My flight was at 10:00a.m. I set my alarm for 8:00a.m. and dozed off. Feeling sunlight in the room, I woke up startled and looked at the clock—which said 9:09a.m.! I was so tired that I slept through my alarm! I knew it would take a Herculean effort to make my 10:00a.m. flight so I did not waste any time. I threw my clothes on, grabbed my bag and sprinted to my car in the hotel parking lot. I sped to the Avis Rental Car facility, dropped off the car and snatched my receipt. I ran to the Avis Shuttle and pleaded with the driver to take me as his only passenger to the American Airlines terminal. I must've looked frantic enough because he accommodated my request. I arrived at the airport at 9:25a.m. I checked in and printed off my boarding pass at an electronic kiosk before sprinting to the security line. I talked my way through most of the security line (again, the frantic look in my eyes must've been convincing enough) and passed through security around 9:40a.m. I then sprinted to my gate and caught the final boarding announcement for my flight back to LGA. Dwayne's comment would prove prophetic—we never did sign Darnell Terrell, but I learned the true meaning of physical and mental perseverance during that unforgettable 24-hour saga, a lesson that has served me well ever since.

As illustrated by the Darnell Terrell trip, recruiting can be likened to a grueling battle of attrition that takes a serious toll on your mind, body and soul—a battle which often becomes a lesson in futility with no successful outcome. For that reason, I always enjoy when I am accompanied on a recruiting trip every so often by my lovely wife, Leslie. Leslie is my icing on the cake. When I meet with players after a game and they see how gracious and beautiful she is, both inside and out, it validates me to a certain extent because they know I must be a halfway decent man to have a good woman like her beside me. To use a football analogy, I outkicked my coverage. In addition to serving as my post-game wing woman, Leslie has proven to be an able-bodied driving partner in the event of an unlikely NYC hurricane.

Leslie and I flew down to Atlanta to attend the Auburn vs. Texas A&M game in late October 2012. I had meetings set up after the game with Daren Bates, former Auburn linebacker and current St. Louis Ram, and Jonathan Stewart, former Texas A&M linebacker who played for a handful of teams during his brief NFL career. It turned out to be a very productive trip because I ended up signing both players, however, Mother Nature had the last word.

It just so happened that our trip coincided with the arrival of Hurricane Sandy in NYC. As I kept abreast of the hurricane's path and projected landfall, I came to the realization that our return flight, scheduled for a 9:00p.m. departure out of Atlanta on Sunday evening, would either be canceled or rescheduled several days later after the hurricane had passed. Not wanting to be stranded in Atlanta for several days with our cat at home fending for himself during the hurricane, I made the executive decision to change our rental car reservation and drive back to NYC from Auburn immediately after the game on Saturday night. After saying our good-byes to Jonathan's parents and Daren's family after the game, Leslie and I hit the road. It was a little after midnight when we left Auburn. I drove the next four hours until we found a room at a Red Roof Inn in Anderson, SC. I set my alarm for 7:00am the next morning and, on 2.5 hours of sleep, Leslie and I hit the road again.

Now, this type of sleep-deprived pilgrimage was old hat for me, but my wife was a trooper. She hung in there with me and even drove a substantial portion of the trip. It ended up being a twenty-hour drive, but we made it back to NYC just in time for Hurricane Sandy. The hurricane hit with destructive force on Monday night and the scariest part of the entire experience was feeling our building sway back and forth. It literally felt like we were on a small dinghy on the high seas. During the most intense wind gusts, we had to have been swaying at least 12 inches each way. As Russell Crowe's Maximus once said, "Death smiles at all of us. All we can do is smile back." Well, we didn't just smile, we laughed. We laughed through the 75 mph wind gusts and the ghostly creaking and swaying of our building. We laughed and we survived. I learned after the fact that tall buildings are engineered to sway and give in high wind. Since we lived on the 15th floor, we definitely bore the brunt of that architectural design. It provided an obvious metaphor for our experience together in starting the sports agency—as a couple we could sway and give, but not break. And sometimes, in this business, you just have to laugh.

The greater question was, would we break as an agency? Or would we be able to recruit and sign enough high-talent, high-character clients to make it work?

Chapter 5

. . . .

A Line in the Sand

"There is no merit to kindness, if you do not have the strength to be mean."

~ French proverb

I am a firm believer that character is cultivated through pain and that by learning to push through any preconceived notions of your own limits, you will not only maximize your God-given genetic code, but you will also develop mental strength and discipline and set yourself apart—in a good way—from those unwilling to pay the price to be great.

Character is defined in the small moments—a cumulative buildup of doing the right thing and making the right choices time and time again. An indomitable spirit is cultivated and strengthened through one's refusal to concede and to see every task—no matter its significance—through to the very end, to the absolute best of your God-given ability.

Discipline and strength of character are traits that definitely come in handy—and are often tested—in the NFL player representation industry, where people often mistake high character for weakness. Nothing can be further from the truth. You can be an upstanding man of faith, integrity and compassion, but you can also be formidable and strong to stand up for what is right. It all comes down to knowing the right time to draw a line in the sand.

Defending your family and friends is one of the most honorable pursuits on this Earth, however, sometimes you won't be the one drawing the line in the sand. It'll be drawn for you when you least expect it. While I was in my second year of law school at Notre Dame, my best friend, Tomas Longo, and I decided to go out for some drinks at the Linebacker Lounge. As any Notre Dame alum can attest, the "Backer" is a staple institution of South Bend, *almost* on par with Notre Dame Stadium and Touchdown Jesus.

It was a Friday evening in February, but the Backer was packed. Tomas and I settled in at the bar and ordered a couple beers. As I took in the sights (off-rhythm dancing), sounds (80s music) and smells (stale beer) of the Backer, Tomas struck up a conversation with a girl seated to his left. A few minutes into their conversation, a guy abruptly steps in between the two of them and bluntly asks the girl, "Hey, why aren't you dancing with me?" After giving him a polite excuse, the guy left and I asked the girl what that was all about. She replied, "He really likes me, but I'm not into him like that. I only want to be friends." Liking Tomas' prospects at that point, I turned away and allowed them to continue their conversation. A couple minutes later, the same guy returned. He was obviously irritated by the fact that the object of his affection was speaking to my friend. He confronted her and angrily asked why she wasn't spending more time with him. At this point, I decided to intervene. "Hey, man, why don't you leave these two alone and mind your own business?" He asked me, "What did you say?" I firmly replied, "Mind your own business." It was at this point, without any further escalation, that the guy started swinging wildly at me. As I put my fists up to cover my face, I instinctively backed up, missing all of his blows.

Thoughts began racing through my mind. "I'm in law school! I can't be getting into a bar fight!" As I managed to evade a few more punches, my train of thought changed drastically. "This guy is really throwing punches at me! Enough is enough! I'm going to knock this guy out." My attacker was tall and skinny so I reflexively reared back—as low as my left hip—and threw the most violent left hook of my life. As I swung through, one of the bouncers, Dave, a friend of mine from the gym, grabbed my assailant and pulled him away from me. Since my punch had already been thrown with ill intent, I couldn't stop the follow-through and I felt a sickening thud when my punch landed above the right eye of a bar patron standing to the left of my attacker. The patron dropped like a sack of potatoes.

It was definitely a case of friendly fire, but I felt awful. As the bouncers jumped in to settle the fracas, the cops were called and my assailant and I were led to the kitchen where we gave our statements. After I had given my statement, Dave, my bouncer friend, came over and reassured me, "Hey bro, I saw it all happen. That guy was throwing punches at you and hit the victim with his elbow!" It was a valiant attempt to protect me from liability, but I knew in my heart of hearts that I had injured an innocent human being. I felt even worse when I learned that my unintentional blow had opened a cut under the bystander's right eyebrow that required stitches.

The next morning, still feeling awful about what had transpired, I called my torts professor, the late Charlie Rice, and asked him if self-defense was a valid legal defense to injury to a third party. Professor Rice pressed me for more information so I reluctantly recounted the events of the previous evening. When I had finished, to my surprise, Professor Rice began laughing. "Hey, you're 1 and 1 now," he chuckled. More than a little confused, I probed further, "What do you mean? Professor Rice, this is Gene Lee." The laughing subsided—just a little. "Oh, Gene! I thought this was Jeevan!" Jeevan was my classmate Jeevan Subbiah who had fought in Bengal Bouts, the campus-wide boxing tournament at Notre Dame that raised money for Bengali charities every year. Professor Rice, as an ex-Marine, was a Bengal Bouts coach and Jeevan, one of his protégés, had lost his first round match the previous year. Despite my angst, I couldn't help but laugh. When we got back to the order of business, Professor Rice scrapped case law and gave me his most basic legal advice. "Don't worry about it. You'll be fine," he reassured me. Oddly enough, those simple words from my legal mentor did the trick. I made a conscious decision not to dwell on the past, but to move forward confidently, armed with the genuine belief that while the outcome wasn't ideal, my intention was noble. I even went back out the next night to the Backer where, coincidentally enough, I had the opportunity to apologize in person to the victim who was in town for her girlfriend's wedding. It turns out Professor Rice was right. Everything worked out fine and nothing ever happened beyond that night (although I did breathe a sigh of relief when the Statute of Limitations expired six years later).

Standing up for your loved ones is an admirable endeavor, however, self-respect is the wellspring of selfless action. You can only stand up for others after you learn to stand up for yourself. Several winters ago, my girlfriend (and now wife)

Leslie surprised me with a long weekend getaway to Turks & Caicos. After months of recruiting, I had just signed our draft class and looked forward to some much needed rest and relaxation. From the moment we got off the plane, it was like a piece of paradise on Earth that I had never before experienced. From the invigorating smell of pristine saltwater to the crystal white sand and majestic blue ocean—at bathwater temperature—Turks & Caicos was the breathtaking backdrop for one of the most memorable vacations of my life.

After lounging on the beach for most of the afternoon and enjoying a quaint dinner at Coco Bistro, Leslie and I decided to immerse ourselves into the local culture. Working off a tip from our waiter, we stumbled upon karaoke night at the local miniature golf course. Leslie is a former Broadway actress and singer/songwriter who can really belt, but I have never been one to shy away from the karaoke mic. After Leslie brought the house down with her rendition of Pat Benatar's "We Belong," I stood up and went with my old standby "The Dance" by Garth Brooks. I had begun karaoking "The Dance" while at Notre Dame and one of the best feelings in the world is to turn people's expectations upside down and reaffirm the time-tested adage that you can never judge a book by its cover. Hearing a young Asian man channel Garth Brooks led to many surprised smiles and a few standing Os at more than a few country bars back in the day! As I began to sing, there were two large black men who—judging by the looks of their facial features, matching polos and size, had to have been twins—felt the need to intermittently let me know that I looked like Jackie Chan (which—no disrespect to Jackie Chan—couldn't have been further from the truth). After ignoring the first few catcalls, I finally lost my patience (I was trying to impress my girlfriend for heaven's sake!) and told them to shut their mouths, which may or may not have been the smartest thing to do given the fact there were several other very large guys in their group.

The catcalls subsided and I finished the song. I managed to regain my composure and led Leslie out to the back patio where we intended to grab a drink. As soon as I stepped on the back patio, another member of the group walked by me and said, "Hey man, you look like Jackie Chan." Without missing a beat, I immediately retorted, "You know what, man, you look like Trevor Berbick." It turns out my choice of doppelganger could not have been more spot on. Trevor Berbick was the former world heavyweight boxing champion whom Mike Tyson beat in 1985 to become the youngest heavyweight champion in history—and this guy really did look like the ex-champ. The entire group erupted in laughter.

After the laughter died down, the smallest guy in the group came over to me with the largest guy in the group who had stayed silent the entire time and asked me, "Do you know who this is?" I didn't know, but braced myself. "This is Michael Moorer—the former heavyweight champ." I looked up at Michael (or "Double," which is short for his nickname "Double M") and straightened myself up, trying my best to exude physical presence in front of the former heavyweight champ. To my surprise, Double still had a big smile on his face from the Trevor Berbick comment (here was a man who definitely caught and appreciated the reference). "Nobody here's going to mess with you man. You stood up for yourself and I respect that." A smile crept across my face as I began to realize and appreciate the sincerity and warmth of this gentle giant.

Double and I immediately struck up a conversation and he lit up when I told him about my line of work. I learned that he was training for his comeback and would be fighting in Hollywood, FL in March. We exchanged numbers and email addresses and kept in contact upon our return to the States. Leslie and I even flew down as his guests to his comeback fight at the Seminole Hard Rock. It was amazing to see such a great friendship develop out of the unlikeliest of situations and it was all because I had the self-confidence and dignity to stand up for myself. Self-respect is not only good for the soul, it will also win you the respect of your peers ... and sometimes even the former heavyweight champ of the world.

Chapter 6

....

My Brother's Keeper

"The time is always right to do what is right."
~ Reverend Martin Luther King, Jr.

The movie Gladiator was on a couple of weeks ago on TNT and, no matter what I'm doing, I'll always stop and watch because for me the movie is a microcosm of life, especially life in the NFL. You have a man, General Maximus, who had everything taken from him. He desperately wanted vindication and justice, but in order to achieve his goal, he knew he needed to make it to Rome as a gladiator. It was kill-or-be-killed, but Maximus continued to win his matches with his eyes transfixed on the ultimate prize which was to rid Rome of the evil Commodus so that democracy would once again reign supreme.

In his quest, Maximus developed a strong bond and love for his fellow gladiators. They formed a strong brotherhood and followed his leadership to defeat their opponents and live to fight another day. They utilized teamwork to the very end until victory had been achieved and Rome finally freed.

Football is the same way. It is a violent sport where

players go to battle each and every day. One man against the other man, best man wins. One man's fear against another man's fear, multiplied by eleven. There is no place to hide on a football field. It's as guttural and primal as it gets. Winners live and continue to fight another day with the hope for future glory. Losers are discarded and tossed by the wayside. These modern day warriors are compensated handsomely for their blood, sweat and tears, but beyond the wealth, celebrity and spoils of fame, players play the game for simple survival. Yet, within each NFL player, there also exists a latent desire to contribute his talents to something greater than himself and, ultimately, win a championship for his legion of men.

The life-or-death nature of a player's existence in the NFL requires the agent-client relationship to be a true brotherhood—a brotherhood that shares the same outlook, goals and "us against them" mindset. A successful agent is in his client's corner and has his back at all times, committing every ounce of his knowledge, expertise and experience to achieving his client's short and long-term goals.

Imagine a job where you are doing stellar work and receiving glowing reviews from your boss or supervisor on a daily basis. However, every Tuesday morning, as you look up from your desk, you see a candidate, impeccably dressed, briefcase and resume in hand, interviewing for your specific position. *Every* Tuesday. That is life in the NFL. Tuesday is an NFL player's day off, but in a twist of cruel irony, it is also the day that teams bring in free agents to workout to take roster spots and jobs. If my clients happen to be in the facility for treatment on a Tuesday, they see a shuttle bus arrive from the airport, out of which pours a few "tryout" hopefuls—guys who were stars in college, and are trying desperately to keep their own NFL dreams alive. They dress and walk out to the practice field, full of nerves and hopefulness eager to snatch the Holy Grail of an NFL job away from another unsuspecting player.

The NFL is a ruthless, cutthroat business and often the only peace a player can find in the chaos is the comfort and reassurance of knowing that he does not need to go it alone.

Brotherhood means you are there for your client through thick and thin. It means you earn your respect over time by being consistent and dependable in your actions and words. As a brother, you share laughter, joy, sorrow and pain. However, brotherhood does not entail being a "yes-man" to your client. Your job requires you to advise your client with honesty and integrity drawing upon your own knowledge, experience and education to give your client a soundly formed opinion, even if it means disagreeing with your client from time to time.

A few years ago, I set up a game watch at a sports bar in NYC for my client Brian Witherspoon. A game-watch is a special event "hosted" by an NFL player in which they get a percentage of the business that their presence brings in. Brian was on IR that season for the New York Giants so he hosted a Monday Night Football event when the Giants played the Saints. I negotiated a percentage of the bar that night for Brian, but the bigger goal was to open the door to a future career in event promotion upon the conclusion of his playing career. The place was packed out that evening and about a week later Brian received a check for a few hundred dollars. Brian called me as soon as he received the check. He was upset at the amount of the check and was under the impression that he was owed more than what he had received. I explained to Brian that not everyone in the bar had paid to be part of his group, but Brian persisted.

After some back and forth, Brian demanded that I contact the bar owner and ask to count bar receipts for the evening. This would not have been a prudent move for many reasons, so I countered, "Spoon, I have no problem asking to see the bar receipts, but I know the owner and really don't think they are short changing you. If I ask to see bar receipts, then they're going to think we don't trust them, which is fine, but you'll need to understand the long-term consequences. You'll burn the bridge not only with this sports bar, but with the other four sports bars this group owns around the city. If your long-term goal is to build a career in event promotion in this town, I don't think this is a wise move." I continued, "For argument's sake, let's say they withheld $2000 in revenues, how much more would you have made off your cut? $200? Is that really worth burning a bridge? Again, I don't think they are withholding anything from you."

There was a long silence as Brian digested what I had just said. He finally relented. "Alright, let's let it go," he replied. Although I had challenged his initial point of view, he came around to see my perspective, respected and, more important, trusted me for having the strength and confidence to advise him with integrity with his best interests in mind. Now, there is a time for being tenacious and going to bat on behalf of your client, but before you take action, you need to step back, analyze the situation and think through all possible outcomes and ramifications to determine the best course of action. There is no value to meaningless puffery in this business. There should be meaning and purpose in every step you take. I can be the hammer, but I want to be swung with meaning and purpose.

Advising your client in this manner requires a certain level of trust that can only be gained over time as your relationship strengthens. An essential part of building the agent-client relationship is attending your client's games throughout the course of the season. This often entails braving the elements and even foregoing traditional holiday festivities. A few years ago, I flew out to Chicago for New Year's Eve to attend a Sunday night game at Soldier Field between the Chicago Bears and Green Bay Packers. I had clients on both teams—Tyler Everett, strong safety for the Bears, and Carlyle Holiday, wide receiver for the Packers—so I figured it would be a great opportunity to visit with both players while I was in town. Shortly after the game ended, I navigated my way through the bowels of Solider Field to see Carlyle off before he hopped on the Packers team bus. After saying good-bye to Carlyle, I then sprinted back through the stadium tunnels to make my way to the family waiting area for the Bears to say hello to Tyler. After catching up with him, I made my way to the remote parking lot across Lakeshore Drive to get my car and find a place to eat. With midnight fast approaching, my options were limited as I drove around town. Realizing that a sit-down meal was not to be, I finally settled on the McDonald's on Clark Street. As the clock struck twelve, I vividly remember revelers walking by and feeling sorry for me, as I sat on my high stool, peering out the window while eating my grilled chicken sandwich. Ironically, that New Year's non-celebration was the one I'll never forget.

Solider Field was the site of another memorable post-game experience. It was the year that the Patriots trounced the Bears in the famous whiteout blizzard game. I attended this game to support my client Sergio Brown, a rookie free safety for the New England Patriots. Sergio was from Chicago, so it was a very meaningful homecoming for him. Now, I'm from northeastern Ohio and attended school for seven years in

South Bend, IN so I'm used to the cold and snow, but, to this day, that was the coldest, most obscenely cold game I have ever attended in my entire life! The snow was coming in droves in blizzard-like conditions and the lake-effect wind was whipping and swirling with no mercy in sight. My toes and fingers were numb. The arctic chill went straight to your bones and I was miserable. Since the game was a blowout, I would've left with most of the Soldier Field crowd if I did not have a client on the visiting team. However, I managed to persevere and brave the elements and immediately after the clock read zeros, I made my way to the visiting buses outside the stadium. As Sergio emerged from the locker room, I congratulated him on his first victory in front of the hometown crowd. Although Sergio had about 35 family members and friends at the game, the fact that his agent stuck around to the very end meant a great deal to him. He was on the field, so he understood that the conditions were brutal, but that's what made my post-game greeting so much more meaningful. In the agent-client relationship, it's often the little things that mean the most.

A couple years later, I had the privilege of having clients on opposing teams in Super Bowl XLVI (Sergio Brown was now a second-year safety for the Patriots while Brian Witherspoon was on IR for the New York Giants). The experience was especially memorable because I was able to secure two tickets—one from Sergio and the other from Brian—to the big game and invite my younger brother David to his very first Super Bowl ever. The Super Bowl was held in Indianapolis that year so I decided to fly out a couple days early to Chicago to check in on a couple of clients training at EFT Performance before driving down to Indianapolis. One of the perks of frequent travel is a preferred rental car account and, sure enough, when I arrived at the Avis Rental Car Center, I had a candy apple red Ford Mustang GT waiting for me with the keys in the ignition. Although the color was a bit flashy for my taste, I loved the car so I didn't give it a second thought as I drove it off the lot.

I spent a couple of productive days in Chicago before departing for Indianapolis on the Saturday afternoon before the game. Having driven to Indy from South Bend before, I had a general idea of which highways to take, so it was to my surprise when my GPS routed me off I-80 West and had me take Exit 14B, which was the Broadway exit for Gary, IN. Having attended Notre Dame for seven years, I had driven past Gary many times before on my way to Chicago. I can still recall the sight of the menacing steel mills and smoke stacks blowing flames and smoke deep into the night as the sky soaked up the gray haze. Gary had gained a nationwide reputation as being one of the hardest, most dangerous cities in the entire country. Imagine my confusion and concern as my GPS began leading me through downtown Gary at 7:00p.m. on a Saturday night…in a candy apple red Ford Mustang!

My pastor once told me that courage is not the absence of fear; courage is overcoming your fear in order to fulfill your God-given purpose. I'm glad that was the definition I was using because my heart was definitely beating at an elevated rate as I drove through downtown Gary that night. It was surreal. Although it was only 7:00p.m., I did not see one person walking around downtown. As I drove past the stadium for the Gary Steelheads, the town's minor-league baseball team, I was routed through an uninviting residential neighborhood where my candy apple red Ford Mustang must've stuck out like a sore thumb. It was at this point that I decided to take control of the situation. Instead of coming to complete stops, I began rolling through stop signs. When I would come to a stoplight, I made sure to give myself a ten-yard cushion before the light in case I needed to hit the accelerator to speed off. After ten very tense minutes, I finally came upon my Holy Grail—a sign for I-65 South. As I sped up the ramp, I exhaled a huge sigh of relief and continued on my way vowing never to trust my Garmin again.

The rest of my trip was relatively uneventful...that is, until I got to Indianapolis. Since my decision to attend the Super Bowl hinged upon having a client in the game, the closest hotel room I could find was in West Lafayette, 65 miles away from downtown Indy. Since Brian had my brother's seat, I had to drive past our hotel to meet up with him in Indy to pick up the ticket. The pre-Super Bowl traffic that night in downtown Indy was absolutely abysmal. As I crawled along at a snail's pace for more than one hour, I noticed that public parking in the downtown area was not to be found. I finally came upon a public parking lot about 2 miles from the action.

Not wanting to miss Brian, I walked hurriedly toward the Westin, where he was waiting for me with my brother's ticket. As I came upon the hotel, motivated by my fear of losing Brian to the pre-Super Bowl festivities, I doubled timed it and began walking with my head down at a furious pace. Out of the corner of my eye, I saw a nicely dressed woman step out of a black car and head toward the hotel entrance. Remembering to be a gentleman, I stopped abruptly to allow her to proceed ahead of me. After she had passed, I began to follow right behind her when the thought occurred to me that she was probably not traveling alone. I did a stutter step and stopped in my tracks. No sooner than I had halted, did a very large man, impeccably dressed with a flat top, march right by me muttering, "Excuse me" in a very menacing tone. I was a little surprised (and slightly agitated after the unforgettable events of the evening) to hear the confrontational undertone. As I entered the hotel, I observed the same man and his wife in the lobby conversing with NFL Network announcer Mike Mayock. I immediately did a double take when I realized the identity of my antagonist. It was Hall of Famer and television analyst Howie Long. I couldn't help but smile and respect his reaction. Here was a man who definitely knew when and where to draw a line in the sand. All in all, the sacrifices I endured that day (mostly caused by the vindictive GPS) were well worth it in the end. My brother and I had a phenomenal time at the game …and I threw my Garmin away when I returned to NYC.

Earning your client's respect is essential in cultivating and strengthening the agent-client relationship. Respect is typically earned through excellence in contract negotiation, endorsement procurement and other professional matters, however, opportunities will arise when you least expect them. Be prepared to rise to the occasion. To prepare for his pre-draft workout at the Notre Dame Pro Day, Sergio trained at EFT Performance, a top-notch training facility located just outside of Chicago. I was out visiting Sergio and had just finished watching him and the rest of their draft-eligible players finish their workout. The players were stretching on the turf and using foam rollers as part of their post-workout recovery routine when Elias Karras, owner of the facility, came up to me and asked, "Hey man, why don't you get a workout in? We'll have Trent put you through a workout." Trent Rogers was a trainer at EFT who at one point held the world record with a 670 lb. bench press. My initial plan was to go back to the hotel and get a workout in later that afternoon, however, I've never been one to shy away from a challenge so I said, "Sure. Why not?" The workout was exactly what you'd expect from a man with a 600+ lb. bench press. There was no rest and my heart rate was elevated the entire time as I lifted under extreme fatigue. As Trent put me through a grueling circuit workout complete with pull-ups, military presses, lateral cable pulls, front deltoid plate raises and kettle bell walks and shrugs, I couldn't help but notice that all of the players, Sergio included, were watching me. However, as tough as the workout was, I did not give in. There was no way I was going to be punked out in front of these players, especially my own client. With all eyes on me, I refused to surrender. Although I was utterly and thoroughly exhausted at the end with nothing left to give, I crushed the workout. I was tired as a dog, but I was glowing for I had gained the respect of Elias, the trainers, the players and, most important, my client Sergio Brown.

A healthy agent-client relationship is not only grounded in the gravitas of personal and professional respect for your stellar work in contract negotiation. You must be able to laugh and share lighter times with your client as well. As one of my first clients from Notre Dame, Lamont Bryant has always been a brother to me. Lamont and I also share a warped sense of humor. The crowning moment occurred while I was visiting Lamont in South Bend before that year's NFL Draft. As we were driving by University Park Mall, I noticed a Fun Tan salon in the plaza off State Route 23. A light bulb went off in my head and I challenged Lamont with the dare of all dares. Never one to back down from a challenge, Lamont accepted. After parking the car, I entered the salon by myself. There was a young lady working behind the counter and I asked her about introductory packages. She handed me a brochure and as I began perusing the brochure, Lamont entered the salon. Lamont walked with purpose to the counter and asked the girl in an earnest tone, "Excuse me, but what kind of specials are you running this month?" I peeked out from behind my brochure and needed to bite my lip, tongue *and* cheek to keep from laughing. Lamont was deadpan serious in his look and the girl was mortified. Here was a 6'4" 275 lb. black man asking her about tanning specials. Although she couldn't grasp why he would want tanning sessions, who was she to question his motives? His serious look and no nonsense nature only reinforced the sincerity of his request. As the poor girl began to meekly rattle off tanning packages, Lamont and I could hold it back no more. We both began convulsing in unbridled laughter. We literally had tears streaming from our faces and the girl, realizing now that it was all a joke, breathed a sigh of relief and began laughing as well. It was an epic moment, and although trivial, inconsequential and downright silly in the grand scheme of things, it did strengthen and solidify our already strong relationship. In addition to being the best medicine, laughter is the glue that bonds an agent-client relationship. A healthy sense of humor is a very powerful tool that you can use to build trust with your client.

And that trust definitely comes in handy when facing the inevitable storms and squalls of life in the NFL. Trust is your tried and true safety net when you are faced with the unpleasant task of delivering bad news to your client. I've had clients cut on Christmas Eve on two occasions and in both instances I've been the one tasked to share the news with my players. The first time occurred when the Chiefs cut Mike Richardson in 2010. Mike ended up getting claimed on waivers by the Indianapolis Colts the next day, but my heart went out to him along with the difficult message I had to convey on Christmas Eve.

The second occasion occurred a couple years later when the New England Patriots cut my client, Jeremiah Warren, a rookie offensive guard from South Florida. Jeremiah's mom had just flown up to visit him for Christmas when I received the call from the Patriots on Christmas Eve. Now, being released on Christmas Eve is hard enough, but having your contract terminated while your mother is in town visiting for Christmas is indescribably cruel. I felt awful when I called Jeremiah to inform him of the news, but he took it with remarkable dignity. I agonized in front of the phone before dialing the number. I took a deep breath.

"Jeremiah, I just got a call from the Patriots and they're letting you go."

"..."

"I can assure you that I will work my tail off to find you your next opportunity," I said. "Unfortunately this is the nature of the business we're in, and unfortunately they don't even stop for Christmas. But don't lose your faith. Lean into God now, and understand that this is a part of a bigger plan that we don't understand." Jeremiah took the news in stride and did his best to stay upbeat. "Ok. Thanks, Eugene. I'll stay ready," he replied.

The day after Christmas I began working the phones like a madman to find Jeremiah his next opportunity.

Jeremiah ended up signing a futures contract with the Arizona Cardinals the next week so it all worked out in the end, but that happy ending did not make my job any easier on the front end. In those unfortunate, yet inevitable, situations that permeate the treacherous landscape of the NFL, trust is what you rely upon to get you through. Trust allows you to cloak any coldhearted communication with compassion, empathy and grace. Trust shields your client from the full brunt of dream destroying NFL reality. Trust emboldens you and your client to persevere and march onward to your next battle as brothers in arms.

I have been blessed to represent many phenomenal clients since my first pickup basketball games at Notre Dame almost two decades ago. However, my all-time favorite client is Brian Witherspoon. Brian and I have endured the full spectrum of life in the NFL. We have shared laughter, tears and every emotion in between. Over the past eight years, we have endured season-ending injuries, waivers, injury settlements, renegotiations and even acts of God.

Ironically enough, our journey to the NFL got off to an inauspicious start. After the conclusion of his season, I flew Brian and his mother up to NYC to sign the necessary paperwork and discuss pre-draft arrangements. As a bona fide foodie, I decided to take them to my favorite Italian restaurant, Gemma in The Bowery Hotel. Gemma offered an extensive menu with traditional Italian favorites including meatballs and pizza. In hindsight, I should've stuck with those more reliable options when asked for a recommendation by Brian's mother. At the time, my favorite dish on the menu was the black squid ink linguini with calamari in a spicy red sauce. So, without any hesitation, I told Brian's mother that she could not go wrong with this dish. Well, what I failed to take into account was the fact that having lived in the culinary mecca of New York City for over ten years, your taste buds expand and learn to go in different directions. They take a culinary backpacking trip through every historic landmark and city in Europe, South America and Asia. Having forgotten the evolution of my gastronomic perspective, I was surprised to see Brian's mother staring blankly at her plate of black pasta after it had arrived. As everyone else dug in to their meals

(Brian included), it finally dawned on me that Brian's mother, being from the South, had probably never before seen black pasta noodles and was completely freaked out by them. I felt awful. As I continued to sneak glances at Brian's mother, her status quo never changed throughout the course of the meal. She continued to stare at her plate, trying to grasp the concept of black noodles. When the waiters finally arrived to clear our plates, she still had not touched hers. To this day, Brian still gives me a hard time about that one.

Brian and I overcame our ominous start and, having celebrated the joy of a breakout rookie campaign for the Jacksonville Jaguars (where he broke the rookie all-purpose yardage record previously held by Maurice Jones-Drew) and persevered through an unexpected end of training camp release by the Carolina Panthers (where he had outplayed several of the younger cornerbacks who had made the final 53 man roster), we found ourselves at a crossroads as training camp began for the New York Giants after the lockout in 2011. We both understood that this was likely Brian's last opportunity in the NFL and that he needed to make the most of it. After the first couple days of camp, I texted Brian to check in on him. He texted me right back to let me know that everything was going great. A couple minutes later, I received another text from Brian, this one with a completely different tone. "Eugene, I honestly feel like a camp body." A camp body is—just like it sounds—a player brought in by a team to round out a training camp roster and provide fodder for scrimmages and drills...but for whom a team has no real plans.

Concerned, I called Brian immediately and he told me the truth. The truth was that he was hardly receiving any reps; that out of eight cornerbacks on the roster, he was Number Eight.

All I could do at this point was impart to Brian my unwavering belief that God has a plan and all you can do is trust in that plan, move forward in faith, work your tail off and do your part. I told Brian that he could only control what he could, but that if he kept his faith, he would eventually get his shot.

And then, a funny thing happened. Bruce Johnson tore his Achilles and was out for the season. Aaron Ross pulled a quadriceps muscle and was out for several weeks. Prince Amukamara, the first round pick for the Giants that year, broke his foot and was out for 8 weeks. Michael Coe hurt his shoulder and was limited in practice as well. As the injuries mounted, Brian's reps increased and he made the absolute most of them. He had receivers such as Hakeem Nicks, Mario Manningham and Victor Cruz on lock and was making plays day after day in practice. He was being praised for his efforts in the media as well. In the first pre-season game against the Carolina Panthers, out of all the defensive backs on the Giants roster, Brian was the only one to grade out with a positive grade. When I spoke with Brian after the game, his spirits were at an all-time high. Not only did he believe he was going to make the team, he felt (and I did as well) that he was going to earn substantial minutes that fall as either the nickel or dime back in their secondary.

As the Giants hosted the Bears in their second pre-season game on Monday Night Football, my wife, my associate Rob and I attended the game to show our support. After seeing Terrell Thomas carted off the field with a torn ACL at the end of the first half, we knew that, despite the unfortunate injury to Terrell, Brian's opportunity was even further in his grasp. Then, it all changed. Early in the third quarter, Brian fielded a punt and cut up the right sideline where he was tackled out of bounds. He was slow to get up and gingerly jogged off the field. Brian headed straight to the trainer's table and I became increasingly concerned as they began to examine and work on his left knee. My concern became a sinking feeling in my stomach when I saw teammate after teammate walk over to Brian to offer words of support, after which he put his head in his hands. Immediately after the game, we waited for Brian in the family area of Met Life Stadium. After what seemed like an eternity, he emerged on crutches with a devastated look on his face. "I have an MRI tomorrow, but the trainer and doctor think it's a torn ACL." My heart sank. After having endured and overcome so much to earn a prominent role in the Giants secondary, the rug was pulled out from under Brian and we were left to ponder what might have been. I knew that Brian should not be alone that evening so instead of dropping him off at the team hotel, my wife, Rob and Brian drove up Route 17 to grab a late post-midnight dinner at the only open establishment within a 10 mile radius, The Meadowlands Diner. After our meal, I dropped Brian off at the team hotel around 3:45am and headed home wondering where the road ahead would lead.

It was later that same week that Hurricane Irene was barreling up the East Coast on a collision course with NYC. After frantic calls from concerned family members, my wife and I decided to take our cat and head up to Woodloch Pines, a resort in the Catskills where my wife had performed as an actor/singer a few years before. Leslie made a call to one of her contacts at the resort and was able to reserve us a sprawling house for the weekend at a discounted rate. Remembering that Brian's fiancée, Ashlee, had flown up to be with him that weekend, I called Brian and relayed my concern about the pending hurricane. I finally convinced Brian to bring

Ashlee and come along with us to escape the devastation. When we picked up Brian and Ashlee at the hotel that Saturday, the wind had started to pick up and I could feel it pushing my car across the road. Little did I know it, but it was a precursor of what was to come. After arriving at the resort, we were treated like royalty. We enjoyed a delicious surf and turf dinner and a show program which was a tribute to the British music invasion of the late 20th century. The rain was coming down in torrents when we hit the sack that evening, but I had a warm sense of satisfaction in knowing that we had evaded the storm's wrath and found safety upstate.

As I drifted in and out of sleep, I couldn't help but notice how hard the wind was howling and whipping. As the intensity of the wind increased, I could hear the house begin to creak and moan with the leaves in the swaying trees sounding like fans cheering on their favorite team. As the morning came, there was a knock on the door. It was a member of the Woodloch staff with a 24 pack of Aquafina water bottles. "We have some power lines down due to some fallen trees so we won't have any electricity or water for a while." The time estimate was a bit misleading. We had no electricity or water for the remainder of our stay. Instead of showering, we used the Aquafina bottles to "bathe" in the bathroom sink. Since we could no longer flush, we made sure we utilized every one of the five bathrooms in our house as well. Nonetheless, Brian, Ashlee, Leslie and I made the most of our circumstances and even enjoyed a candlelight dinner (which was the only light in the dining room) before heading back to NYC the following morning, (the return trip took three times longer than normal due to detours to avoid flooding and fallen trees caused by the hurricane's windy swath of destruction) so I could drop off Brian at the Giants facility for pre-surgery rehab on his knee. Ironically, we had left NYC to escape the hurricane's wrath, but while Hurricane Irene proved to be nothing more than a strong rainstorm in NYC, the windy aftermath had left us without power or water upstate. It is often said that the best laid plans of mice and men often go awry, but I would never trade my Hurricane Irene experience (even the lack of electricity and running water) for enduring this unexpected, at times comical, adversity together was the glue that would cement our relationship. The unforgettable events of that weekend would bond Brian and me beyond football, beyond career-ending injuries, and beyond agent-client, as true brothers for life.

Chapter 7

....

Growing Pains

"Self-respect is the fruit of discipline; the sense of dignity grows with the ability to say no to oneself."
~ Abraham Joshua Heschel

I decided to start my own agency because of the freedom to create and build something from the ground up according to my own principles. I loved the challenge and reward of imprinting every aspect of my organization with my own philosophy, core values and ideals. I have walked my path in this industry with purpose, confidence and humility, but it's not to say there weren't some pitfalls along the way.

I have always lived by the adage that how a man dresses tells the world how he feels about himself. I may have taken that credo a little too far during my first pro day experience at Notre Dame. I was still practicing law at the time and the firm dress code was suit and tie every day. So, when I showed up for Deveron Harper's pro day workout wearing a three piece pinstriped suit, I merely thought I was dressing for success. Little did I know that my choice of attire became a fashion statement as loud as wearing a tank top to a wedding.

Mickey Marotti was the head strength-and-conditioning coach at Notre Dame at the time. He is now the head strength-and-conditioning coach at Ohio State and Urban Meyer's secret weapon in developing SEC-type speed and fast-twitch explosiveness in the Midwest. Mick's policy at the time was that no agents were allowed in the facility to watch the pro day workout and he enforced that rule to the fullest extent. So, as I milled around the lobby of Loftus (Notre Dame's indoor training facility), all decked out in my three piece suit, I waited anxiously for the conclusion of the workout so I could find out how Deveron performed. He ended up having an excellent day. He ran and jumped well and looked smooth in his positional drills. Deveron tested so well that he was the subject of a feature story in the South Bend Tribune the very next day. Although the article was primarily about Deveron's stellar workout, there was a mention at the end of the article of "one agent decked out in a three piece suit" who came up to Deveron after the workout to solicit him into signing. Looking back, I must've fit the agent stereotype to a tee!

Beyond my fashion faux pas, I have learned the hard way that, as difficult as it may be, you need to draw a line with your client and refuse to take any action that could jeopardize your own financial health. Over time, as you earn your client's trust, sometimes the line between agent and family becomes blurred, so you need to set a boundary when it comes to risking your own creditworthiness. One of the biggest mistakes I made when I first started in the industry was co-signing a car loan for a client fresh out of college. Although my client did not end up making the NFL, he played in the CFL for a couple seasons before entering the business world. I did not think anything of the car loan until I received a call from my client's mother several years later apologizing profusely while informing me that my client missed two consecutive car payments. Sure enough, when I checked my credit the next day, there were two 60 day late payments on my report and my score was dinged significantly. Although I am still very close with this client, I will never again cosign any type of secured debt instrument in my role as an agent.

As my agency started to grow, I began to grasp the concept of economies of scale, and slowly realized that I could only do so much. I knew that I would always be constrained as a one-man operation (especially in recruiting) by the simple fact that I could only be in one place at a time. In order for me to expand and achieve my goals within the NFL player representation industry, I needed to assemble the right team.

Much of my initial growth occurred organically. I met my first associate, Derrick, while speaking at a sports law symposium at St. John's Law School. Derrick was a first-year law student at the time and was extremely persistent in following up after my talk. He sent me his resume and numerous follow-up emails requesting a quick meeting to pick my brain and learn more about the industry. There was authenticity and a tenacious, yet tactful, nature about his approach…and it worked. His persistence won me over. I brought him on board as an intern, then as an associate and, finally, as a certified NFLPA contract advisor. I poured all of my knowledge and experience into training and developing him into a bona fide recruiter and agent who would go on to become a tremendous asset for my agency.

In a similar vein, I met another member of my team and my good friend, Eugene Egdorf, one of the top litigation attorneys in the country and a certified NFLPA contract advisor, while speaking on a sports law panel at Fordham Law

School. Although Gene's specialty was (and is) sports litigation (he negotiated the $40 million EA Sports settlement on behalf of current and former NCAA athletes), he would always find time to assist in recruiting and legal counseling for our clients. Dwayne Harper was the older brother of one of my first clients, Deveron Harper, and I initially brought Dwayne in to train a defensive back client from Ohio State. In addition to being Deveron's older brother, Dwayne was an All-Pro cornerback with the Seattle Seahawks and San Diego Chargers during his twelve-year NFL career and was named to the Sports Illustrated All-NFL team of the '90s. Dwayne enjoyed the teaching and mentoring aspect of his limited engagement so much that I asked him to come on board as my Director of Player Development.

In later years, I made a much more conscious effort to identify, secure and develop the right talent. I always looked for someone who had what I liked to call the "Warhol Effect." Andy Warhol was a legendary artist who would take normal everyday objects such as Campbell's Soup cans and potted plants, infuse them with splashes of vibrant colors and elaborate color schemes and convert them into one-of-a-kind, brilliant masterpieces. People who have the "Warhol Effect" possess the innate creativity, courage and confidence to take an ordinary assignment and stamp it with their own unique brand of excellence—to add unforeseen value to a project, to build a better mousetrap (on their own volition) and to take the mundane and make it masterful. For me, the "Warhol Effect" is a nonnegotiable job requirement and each one of my hires—from law school graduates to Hollywood talent agency interns to former college football players—has possessed it in spades.

With my team assembled, one of the first opportunities we

had to recruit as a group came at Ohio State Agent Day. Ohio State used to be one of the few schools that held an agent day after their annual spring game. Ohio State Agent Day was an extremely well-run event that took place in Ohio Stadium. Under the agent day format, each agency was required to submit a list of players whom they wanted to meet beforehand to the compliance department. If there was mutual interest on behalf of the player, the meeting would then be scheduled. Each agency was assigned their own luxury box and each player meeting would last 30 minutes before the player and his parents would move on to their next meeting.

Our whole team was there that year and we were poised for some very productive meetings because we were representing Ohio State defensive back Tyler Everett at the time. One of the players whom we had requested was a defensive tackle by the name of David Patterson. He was a good football player, but his nickname alluded to another distinguishing characteristic. "Oh, you guys are meeting with Bad Body Dave?" Tyler asked when I ran through the player list with him. Apparently, that was the nickname bestowed upon David by his teammates after several years of locker-room familiarity. It was also one of the funniest nicknames I had ever heard, right up there with Uncle Mike.

After committing myself to wiping that nickname completely out of my head, we sat down with David's mother and his uncle. David's mother was a mortgage broker wearing a Bluetooth earpiece and his uncle was dressed like he was straight out of a Kool Moe Dee video from the early '80s. He was wearing a white Kangol beach hat, baby-blue satin jumpsuit, white Nike high tops and enough gold chains to make Mr. T proud. The meeting started well. I discussed all aspects of our representation package, from the credentials of our management team to the unparalleled service offered and personalized attention we would provide. About halfway through the meeting, David's uncle, who had been listening intently and remained silent the entire time, piped up. "David loves football, man. He has such a passion for the game. He LOVES the game. In fact, he loves football so much that every weekend he helps me pick the over/under on all of these college games."

The room went radio silent. I glanced over quickly at Dwayne Harper who I could tell was biting his lip, trying not to laugh. Realizing the show must go on, I nodded my head in agreement and replied, "Yes, that takes quite a bit of love and knowledge for the game. You must be proud." Our meeting wrapped up shortly thereafter as Ms. Patterson and David's uncle exited for their next meeting in the luxury box next to ours. We had a 30-minute break before our next meeting so Dwayne, Derrick and myself congregated in the hallway outside our room. After a couple of minutes, David's uncle emerged from the meeting next door, quickly sought out Dwayne (the only black member of our entourage—as Dwayne duly noted, "he went straight to the brother in the group") and began to carefully retrace his steps. "Hey, bro, when I said David helps me pick the games, he doesn't actually bet on them. He just does it for fun, man! He doesn't make any money off of it! Just for fun! You know how it is, bro." Dwayne nodded his head in affirmation and quickly responded, "I got you, bro! I got you. It's all good." They embraced in a bro hug and David's uncle went back into his meeting. No sooner than he had departed, did Dwayne declare, "He's signing with us." I was utterly perplexed and still in shock over what I had just seen. "How do you know?" I asked. "Because we've got something on him now," Dwayne deadpanned. Touché.

Although we didn't sign Bad Body Dave, I enjoyed the camaraderie of my team over the next few years as we continued to grow the agency. Each one of us had different strengths and personality traits, but the whole was definitely greater than the sum of its parts and our client list began to grow as a result. Alas, all good things must come to an end. Around the filming of "The Dotted Line," I decided to part ways with my protégé, Derrick, due to some philosophical differences that were manifested at the Combine that year. He had grown and matured into a top-notch NFL agent, but his desire to captain his own ship became increasingly clear in Indianapolis and the pursuit of his own agenda was causing a divide within my agency. So, after much thought, soul-searching and prayer, I came to the gut-wrenching conclusion that it was best for us to go our separate ways. Although the split was amicable, sitting down at the Cipriani in Grand Central to deliver the news to Derrick in person was one of the more difficult tasks I've ever had to face in my entire professional career. We had spent seven years together and I definitely appreciated his loyalty (especially in an industry where loyalty is often an uncommon trait). I had watched him grow from a law school intern to an established, successful agent and that was extremely fulfilling for me to see, even after our split. Less than two years later, I was forced to terminate another associate who, after a promising start, had revealed himself as a serious threat to the agency brand I had worked so hard to build. This associate worked hard, but played even harder, to the point where the decisions he was making while "off the clock" were beginning to undermine my own reputation and credibility. Although terminating a member of your team is never an easy or enviable task, if it is necessary for the continued growth of your agency consistent with its foundational mission, it must be done. Sometimes you need to prune a tree so it can continue to grow.

The flip side is no fun either. Unfortunately for me, the most documented client termination in my career took place on ESPN. Although I was extremely angry and upset at the time for what I felt was an uninformed and unjustified termination by Jacquian, I did manage to learn some lessons as a result. I felt betrayed after having invested thousands of dollars to fund Jacquian's pre-draft training with no commission to show as a result. I could not fathom how a client could turn his back on someone who had taken a chance and believed in him at a time when no other agent would. Although my outrage dissipated over time, the moral of the story became ingrained in my subconscious. I learned to be much more proactive in checking with my clients on a regular basis and asking them pointed questions about their finances, family and health to make sure that they knew, beyond a shadow of a doubt, that I was in their corner at all times. I could no longer assume that everything was fine just because my client didn't mention anything to me. From this moment forward, I would be proactive and delve at the source. I learned to require each one of our draft-eligible clients to sign a pre-draft expense reimbursement agreement which would obligate them to repay all pre-draft training expenditures should they choose to terminate our services before the negotiation of their first NFL player contract (I call this one the Jacquian Williams rule). Although the termination was a tough pill to swallow (especially on national TV), I believed in God's plan and was committed to grow from this experience and become an even better agent down the road. Everyone makes mistakes, but fools make the same ones over and over again. I would not be the court jester.

Although losing a client to termination is painful, it is nearly as gut-wrenching to come in a close second on players whom you have recruited throughout the course of the year. The draft-eligible recruiting cycle entails a significant commitment of time and resources to travel and meet with players and their families from April through the end of the year. Beyond the monetary and opportunity costs involved, successful recruiting also requires a deep-rooted emotional investment in each player whom you recruit. You must commit fully to the process and invest every ounce of energy in your mind, body and soul to signing your player. You must have the strength, courage and endurance to fight against dozens of other agents to be the one left standing at the end of the grueling battle. After sacrificing so much and leaving everything you have on the field of play, there is an indescribable emptiness that consumes your entire being when you come in second place. It is equivalent to running an entire marathon only to arrive at the finish line exhausted, but with not a soul in sight, no one to cheer you on or recognize your accomplishment, just utter, eerie and haunting silence.

In the NFL player representation industry, there are no moral victories for second place and, try as you might, you never forget the ones that got away. From players such as Justin Tuck to Miles Austin to Rex Burkhead, my agency has had its share of heart-wrenching recruiting losses over the past decade, but through the pain and adversity of coming in second, I have learned one infallible, absolute truth—the hand of God is always at work. Nowhere was this more evident than during my recruitment of Ohio State linebacker Marcus Freeman. Entering his senior season, Marcus was a highly touted player with a first round draft grade. We connected immediately due to our shared Korean heritage (Marcus' mother was Korean and his father was black) and his recruitment went like clockwork. Marcus was (and is) a man of integrity and faith and as I got to know him better, I was convinced that not only was he the perfect fit for my agency, he was going to be our marquee first round pick, a player around whom the agency could continue to grow and be built.

After our initial meeting at agent day, I attended a couple Ohio State games that fall before sitting down with Marcus and his father for final agent meetings after the Michigan game. Marcus met with four agencies (mine included) and there were some heavy-hitters in the bunch, but despite the tough competition, I came away from our meeting feeling that I had brought it home and that there was no other choice for Marcus, but to sign with me. I was extremely diligent in my follow up over the next few weeks sending Marcus a detailed pre-draft timeline along with real-time feedback from NFL scouts. As I departed NYC for Christmas with my family in Ohio, I knew it was only a matter of time before I would receive the official commitment. I finally heard from Marcus on Christmas Eve, but it was *not* the news I was expecting to hear. "I talked it over with my dad and we've decided to go in a different direction," Marcus explained. I was utterly devastated. I graciously wished Marcus all the best in his future endeavors and quickly hung up the phone, trying desperately to figure out some sort of Plan B for myself and my agency.

Resilience is one of my defining traits, but it was a little different this time around. As hard as I tried to bounce back, I just couldn't shake the tinge of sadness and emptiness that infiltrated my Christmas spirit that year. Little did I know that I was being taught an invaluable lesson in faith and trust that holiday season. Marcus Freeman, through no fault of his own, ended up being drafted by the Chicago Bears in the fifth round that spring, thus reducing his signing bonus to *1.5%* of the average signing bonus for a first round pick. At the end of the pre-season, Marcus was cut by the Bears. He was signed by the Buffalo Bills to their practice squad in late September before being released in early October. Marcus was then signed by the Houston Texans to their practice squad in early November. A few months later, during a routine pre-season physical, Marcus was diagnosed with an enlarged heart condition and was forced to retire from the NFL. There was a happy ending to this story, however. Although his NFL career ended abruptly, Marcus found his calling in coaching and mentoring young men. As the linebackers coach for Purdue University, Marcus is quickly building a reputation as one of the rising stars in the college football coaching ranks.

With the lucid perspective offered by distance and time, I realize now that if I had signed Marcus Freeman and made the requisite financial investment commensurate with a projected first round pick, my actual commission would not have even made a dent in the upfront expenses. The unrecouped financial outlay would've proven devastating to my agency! Although I was certain that signing Marcus Freeman was going to be the catalyst for the future growth and success of my agency, in hindsight, I was dead wrong. I could only see a few miles down the road, but that was nothing compared to an eternal vantage point, one that could see as far down the road as it would lead (and several billion miles beyond). The ones that got away really weren't the ones that got away because they were all part of a greater plan for my future— one filled with prosperity and hope. All I needed to do was trust in God.

Chapter 8

....

Never Say Die

"Fall down seven times, get up eight."
~ *Japanese Proverb*

The NFL player representation industry is an unlit, unmarked road filled with bumps, potholes and dangerous hairpin turns. In order to succeed in this industry, you need the flexibility, creativity and perseverance to navigate this road like a NASCAR driver in order to overcome unforeseen obstacles as they arise. Improvisational skills are a prerequisite for the job.

You must approach the job like a gung-ho Marine— willing to improvise, adapt and overcome. Semper Fi was on display during the pre-draft workouts for two former college quarterback clients of mine who would go on to make the transition to wide receiver in the NFL.

Carlyle Holiday was the starting quarterback for Notre Dame during Tyrone Willingham's magical first season (when Notre Dame rose all the way to a #3 ranking and beat a heavily favored Florida State team in Tallahassee). After a couple rough seasons, Carlyle became the scapegoat for ND's offensive struggles and Brady Quinn came in to take over the offense. In an effort to showcase his prodigious athletic skills and salvage his shot at an NFL career, Carlyle switched to wide receiver for his senior season. Unfortunately, Carlyle did not receive the playing time that he anticipated or warranted that fall, so with limited game film at wide receiver, his pre-draft workouts took on the utmost importance that spring. Shortly before the Notre Dame Pro Day, Carlyle tweaked his hamstring in training and was unable to run his forty at the pro day workout.

Knowing that NFL teams would salivate over a 6'3" 215 lb. wide receiver with sub 4.5 speed (which is what Carlyle would've run), I knew it was imperative for Carlyle to have an official forty time on record before the NFL Draft. So, three weeks after the pro day, when his hamstring was close to 100%, I hit the phones to schedule an individual workout for Carlyle at Notre Dame. With the NFL Draft fast approaching, the turnout was sparse, but the Patriots and Colts were in attendance with stopwatches in hand. When I arrived at the Notre Dame indoor training facility on the morning of Carlyle's workout, I was told by the director of football operations that Carlyle could not use the facility for his individual workout due to spring football practice that afternoon. The edict made no sense to me and while I argued my point vehemently, it slowly occurred to me that Carlyle was Bob Davie's recruit who had played under Tyrone Willingham and to whom new coach Charlie Weis had no affiliation or allegiance.

Realizing that my argument was falling upon deaf ears, I wasted no more time. I gathered Carlyle and the NFL team reps and headed straight to the intramural soccer fields nearby. It was a bright sunny day with a slight breeze carrying the all-too-familiar scent of Ethanol across the Notre Dame campus. The conditions were ideal for an outdoor workout…or so I thought. When we arrived at the fields, my jaw dropped in horror. The fields were used for intramural soccer and the lack of varsity competition and upkeep had led to their demise. There were ruts and holes all over and the grass was uncut and matted down in a post winter shade of brown and yellow.

Realizing that we had no choice, I, along with the help of Nick Caserio, Director of Player Personnel for the New England Patriots, scouted out the flattest, rut-free portion of grass for Carlyle's forty. Carlyle ran a good time considering the conditions (in the high 4.6 range) and ended up running routes and catching passes for nearly thirty minutes. This was the first time I had ever met Nick and I was shocked by the strength of his arm. He was throwing bullets left and right, but Carlyle was up to the task and caught almost every ball thrown his way. I later found out that Nick was a college quarterback at John Carroll where he played with current Patriots offensive coordinator, Josh McDaniels, who was his wide receiver. Although the conditions were far from ideal, we made the most of our circumstances and Carlyle would go on to a four-year NFL career. He even found himself in the NFL record books by catching Brett Favre's record-breaking 4,968[th] career completion (breaking the mark previously held by Dan Marino) for the Green Bay Packers.

Carlyle's success emboldened me to represent another college quarterback attempting to make the transition to wide receiver in the NFL. Eddie McGee was a 6'3" 210 lb. athlete from the University of Illinois who had served as Juice Williams' backup before converting to wide receiver before his senior season. Eddie was extremely athletic and fast (he would run a 4.46 at his pro day), but similar to Carlyle, he had limited game film and reps at wide receiver during his senior season. His pro day workout would be extremely important in determining the extent of his opportunity at the next level. It was the year of the lockout so I knew that contacting the NFL teams in attendance would be the key to securing Eddie the best opportunity with the right NFL team. When I arrived at the Illinois football office that morning to pick up a pass for Eddie's fiancée, I was told that the pro day was off limits to agents and that only family members would be allowed in to watch. This was discouraging because I knew what I needed to do for Eddie; how I wanted to market him to the right people as a projected position switch with the speed, tools and intellect to make the conversion to wide receiver in the NFL. However, the agent prohibition was only a speed bump, not a roadblock. Semper Fi!

As the receptionist got up to get the family pass, I glanced down on her desk and noticed a sign-in sheet for every NFL scout, coach, personnel director, college scouting director and GM in attendance. Realizing my window of opportunity was fleeting, I began looking around feverishly to find a pen and a piece of paper. As my mind began to process the actual time required to jot down the necessary information, I realized that I simply would not have enough time. And then it dawned on me. Use your Blackberry camera! I pulled out my Blackberry and discreetly took a photograph of that sign-in sheet. It turned out to be one of the best photos I had ever taken— crisp, in focus and with every name and NFL team clearly legible. I referred back to my sign-in sheet photo after the pro day and was able to follow up with those teams in attendance who had a need and personnel fit at wide receiver for a player of Eddie's size, speed and skillset. Eddie would go on to a two-year stint with the Oakland Raiders ... and the catalyst for his NFL career was a seldom-used Blackberry camera.

Ironically, it was also a camera (of the video variety) that allowed me to jumpstart another client's NFL career. Jacquian Williams was an off-the-radar NFL prospect entering his senior season at USF with no National or BLESTO grades (National and BLESTO are the two scouting services used by a majority of NFL teams). He had started one game during his junior season after transferring from Fort Scott JUCO. Although he enjoyed a productive senior campaign exhibiting NFL-caliber playmaking ability and sideline-to-sideline speed for a weakside linebacker, he played the season at 216 lbs. in the Big East and was an afterthought in most NFL Draft circles (as evidenced by the lack of an all-star game or Combine invite). Not one to follow consensus opinion, I decided to go back to the tape and I liked what I saw.

I contacted my good friend Mark Sadowski, southeast scout for the Chicago Bears at the time, and asked him about Jacquian. Mark gave me his honest opinion. "He does have some ability, but for him to have a shot at the next level, he'll need to gain at least 15 lbs. and maintain his speed." Armed with that information, I decided to take a chance and sign Jacquian—and we set out to shock the world. Jacquian trained, ate and supplemented religiously for eight weeks at EFT Performance in Chicago and when he showed up in Tampa for the USF Pro Day on an idyllic south Florida day—clear, sunny, 75 degrees and no humidity—I knew the conditions were ideal for him to throw down a monster workout. I was ready as well, armed with DVDs of Jacquian's three best games from his senior season. I knew that after Jacquian's workout, teams would be clamoring for his game film and I wanted to be prepared to strike while the iron was hot.

Instead of allowing NFL teams to arbitrarily pick games to watch, I wanted to take control of the evaluation process and force teams to grade Jacquian at his ceiling (which would in turn maximize his draft slot) by providing them convenient access to game film that would showcase him playing at his highest level. The pro day started with measurements, jumps and bench in the USF weight room. After numbers were compiled, NFL personnel, family members, agents and players headed to the USF track and soccer stadium. The only number with which I was concerned was Jacquian's weight so as I made my way to the stadium, I tracked down a USF staffer and asked him for the goods. He replied, "231 lbs." My eyes lit up at the news and I picked up the pace in eager anticipation of what was yet to come. When I arrived at the stadium, I was told by a USF staffer that only NFL personnel were allowed on the grass infield (which was where the forty would be run and all other drills would take place) and that family members, agents and friends would need to sit in the stands to watch the workout. As I grudgingly trudged up the stadium stairs, I found a seat in the first row. The infield was teeming with NFL personnel and while the physical distance between where I was sitting and the infield was probably only twenty yards, it felt as if I was on another continent.

The infield was an NFL networking goldmine and I knew that I had to find a way down to that field to market Jacquian to the fullest and leverage his workout into the best possible NFL opportunity. Out of the corner of my eye, I noticed a camera crew from the local television station making their way to the stadium. I quickly exited my seat and milled around the outside stadium gate and waited for them to pass by. As they walked by, I quickly fell into step on the left shoulder of the cameraman holding my iPad tightly against my chest with my pen in my other hand. Now, I may or may not have looked like a television reporter walking in with my crew, but as I easily made my way past the USF staffer, I decided to let sleeping dogs lie and allow him to make his own assumption.

As I made my way on to the infield, I was immediately spotted by my good friend Jerry Angelo, general manager for the Chicago Bears. I had been in touch with Jerry regularly on Jacquian leading up to the pro day so it was satisfying to know that my credibility was being validated. He greeted me warmly. "Eugene, your guy's having a helluva workout," he exclaimed. Jerry then called over two members of the Chicago Bears coaching staff, Head Coach Lovie Smith and defensive line coach Rod Marinelli, and introduced me to both of them.

I spent the next twenty minutes working the crowd and handing out DVDs of Jacquian's game film. As I had predicted, the game film went like hotcakes. It was a "Who's Who" of NFL personnel on the infield. In addition to Jerry, Tim Ruskell (long-time Seahawks and Bears executive), Bill Belichick (Head Coach of the New England Patriots), Phil Emery (Director of College Scouting for the Kansas City Chiefs and future General Manager for the Chicago Bears), Lake Dawson (Vice President of Player Personnel for the Tennessee Titans) and Jason Licht (Personnel Executive for the New England Patriots and current General Manager for the Tampa Bay Buccaneers) were all there intently watching the workout...and Jacquian put on a show. He blazed a 4.52 forty on natural grass (at 231 lbs.) and looked like a smooth shutdown cornerback in his position drills. He did not drop one ball! Toward the end of the workout, I was finally spotted by a USF staffer who asked if I was media. I answered him with a befuddled look on my face and told him I was not. He then told me that only NFL personnel and media were allowed on the infield and that I needed to leave immediately—which was totally fine with me because at this point, my work was done.

I exited the infield quickly and inconspicuously and made my way to the outside of the stadium gate where I spent the next twenty minutes handing out DVDs to the handful of NFL scouts, coaches and personnel directors whom I had missed on the infield. One of the last people to exit the stadium was Jerry Angelo. As Jerry made his way through the stadium gate, he spotted me again, shook his head, smiled and rhetorically asked, "How come I knew you would be the only agent out on that field?" There was a level of respect in Jerry's comment for he knew that I had done right by my client; that I had found a way to get the job done in spite of the adverse circumstances and, most importantly, that I had done it with class. I smiled, shook his hand and was off to celebrate with my client (Jacquian would go on to five official pre-draft visits with NFL teams), all the while basking in the radiant warmth of the setting south Florida sun and incandescent glow of victory attained.

A far cry from the south Florida sun was the blizzard that hit the Northeast in late February 2010. The blizzard wreaked havoc on airline travel plans and coincided with the start of the NFL Scouting Combine in Indianapolis. I was representing Sergio Brown, an unheralded safety from Notre Dame who, despite being a special teams demon for all four years, had only started in the base defense for the last half of his senior season. I was looking forward to the Combine as a tremendous opportunity to market Sergio to NFL teams and raise his draft stock. Sergio did not receive a Combine invite so it was imperative for me to set the plate for scouts with the Notre Dame Pro Day fast approaching. Knowing what I needed to do for Sergio, I was a little concerned when I received a call from Delta informing me that my original flight to Indianapolis for Thursday afternoon had been canceled and rescheduled for Friday morning. My concern turned to crisis when I received a call later that day informing me that my Friday morning flight had been canceled too and that I was now rescheduled for Saturday morning.

Knowing that I could not lose precious time in Indianapolis, I began scrambling to find an alternate means of transportation. I checked the Amtrak train schedule, but the 26 hour ride would've defeated the purpose. I thought about driving my own car to Indianapolis, but quickly nixed that idea when I thought about the 12 hour return trip on Sunday evening. Then, it occurred to me. I could take a one-way rental car to Indianapolis, call Delta and keep my return flight to LaGuardia on Sunday evening. The only perceived obstacle was the weather, but having grown up and attended school in the Midwest, I dismissed the blizzard as nothing more than a snow day and booked my travel arrangements.

It was 9:00p.m. on Thursday evening when my associate Drew and I took a cab from my apartment and headed to JFK airport to pick up our rental car. The snow was coming down in torrents and beginning to accumulate on the roads. As our taxi navigated the roads at 15 mph, I began to realize just how treacherous conditions truly were. It took us nearly two hours to get to the Avis Rental Car Center at JFK and when we finally arrived, I was forced to make an executive decision. Rent the car, drive off into the night and brave whatever blizzard-like conditions lay ahead, or, hop back in the taxi, head back home and concede to the elements. I thought long and hard about our safety, the warmth of my apartment and the treacherous roads that lied ahead. But, then I thought about Sergio, overlooked during his four-year career at Notre Dame, training his tail off for his one opportunity to shine at his pro day, longing for just one shot at the NFL. All of a sudden, my decision became clear. I looked at Drew and asked him if he was on board to take the trip. Without any hesitation, Drew nodded in affirmation. We were off to Indy.

I drove the first four hours of the trip. I had never before experienced hazardous roads like the ones I encountered that night. Luckily for us, we were given a heavier car (a Chrysler 300), however, I still couldn't go faster than 15 mph without feeling my tires start to slip on the snow-blanketed surface. When we stopped for gas in southern New Jersey around 4:30am, we had only gone fifty miles. Drew took the wheel when we got back on I-78. Other than the occasional rig, I noticed that we were the only passenger vehicle on the road and my heart began to sink. Trying not to second guess my decision, I forced myself to stay positive and, with adrenalin flowing, I committed to staying awake to support Drew. It's a good thing I did. About thirty minutes into Drew's segment, conditions deteriorated rapidly. Noticing that I could only see white ahead of me, I looked to Drew who was death-gripping the steering wheel with both hands. Staring straight ahead, Drew anxiously sought my guidance. "Eugene! Eugene! I can't see anything ahead," he exclaimed. Knowing that there was no traffic in our immediate vicinity, my #1 goal was to keep the car on the road—even if it was straddling the center line. The first step in accomplishing that objective was to keep Drew calm.

"Stay cool. We're going to be fine. There's no one else out here," I reassured Drew with my heart pounding through my chest. Necessity is the mother of invention and, similarly, the human desire for self-preservation was what prompted Drew to devise the brilliant idea of centering the car by looking out his driver's side window to gauge the distance to the concrete median. We endured whiteout conditions for the next twenty minutes as we trudged along I-78. The rest of the trip was relatively uneventful as the snow dissipated in the early morning hours and we arrived safely (and exhausted) in Indianapolis around 2:30p.m. the following afternoon. I spent the next three days handing out game film and information on Sergio to NFL scouts, coaches, personnel directors and GMs in attendance. He never truly understood the sacrifice we made, but, in hindsight, I would put myself in harm's way all over again because it was necessary for my client to earn his shot and maximize this once in a lifetime opportunity. Sergio Brown would go on to use the foundation we laid in Indianapolis to build a six-year NFL career.

That's not to say the road ahead was easy for Sergio. He followed up our Combine prelude with a dazzling pro day performance. He ran a 4.44 which is a blazing time for a safety with prototypical size (6'1" 212 lbs.). On the heels of his monster workout, we entered the draft thinking there was a reasonable chance he could get selected in the seventh round. Sure enough, the Cowboys, Broncos and Patriots came calling in the final round to indicate their interest in *possibly* selecting Sergio with their final pick.

Unfortunately, none of those teams pulled the trigger and as soon as "Mr. Irrelevant" (the final pick in the NFL Draft) had been announced, my phone lines started ringing off the hook. I received phone calls from eight different NFL teams trumpeting their opportunity for Sergio as an undrafted free agent all the while pressing me hard for a time-sensitive commitment (before they would move on to the next guy on their list). Fortunately, I had done my homework and was prepared for the onslaught. Having charted all 255 picks of the entire draft, I knew which safeties had been drafted by which teams, and in which rounds. I had also compiled real-time depth charts and free agent signings for all 32 NFL teams, along with a statistical report from the NFLPA documenting the percentage of undrafted free agents, by NFL team, which had made final 53 man rosters the previous year. After analyzing the available data, the decision was clear. We were signing with the New England Patriots.

New England had not drafted a safety, they had a mid-level veteran safety on their roster, James Sanders, whose backup/special teams role was one Sergio could easily fill at half the cost. Their new defensive backs coach, Corwin Brown, was Sergio's defensive coordinator at Notre Dame the year before, and (this was the kicker), fifty percent (50%!) of their undrafted free agents had made the final 53 man roster the year before. This was by far the highest percentage in the NFL. After talking everything over with Sergio and his mom and making sure we were all on the same page and 100% secure in our decision, I went on to negotiate the highest undrafted free agent signing bonus that the Patriots had given to a player in the previous two seasons.

Sergio dominated OTAs, training camp and the pre-season and entered the final pre-season game running with the "1s" on three out of four special teams units. His roster spot was secure...or so we thought. The NFL cut down deadline occurred two days after the final pre-season game on Saturday of Labor Day weekend. Cut down day is the only time you *never* want to hear from a client. In an effort to take my mind off matters, I took my wife to watch some epic tennis at the US Open. As the final day session match concluded and the 4:00p.m. EST deadline passed, I still had not heard from

Sergio. I exhaled a sigh of relief and Leslie and I made our way toward the park exit. Before leaving, we decided to make a slight detour to check out the Chase-sponsored interactive tennis exhibit. There was a station where you could test your serve speed so I hopped into line. Shortly after noticing that I was the oldest person in line by at least 25 years, my cell phone rang. It was Sergio. He had just gotten a call to bring his playbook and come see Coach Belichick. It turns out that Sergio had made the final 53 man roster, but the Patriots had made a last-minute trade for Kansas City Chiefs safety Jarrad Page, who was essentially the same player as Sergio (backup safety, special teams demon), albeit with three more years of NFL experience.

Sergio was devastated, but I knew this was par for the NFL course and that it was time for me to go to work. Suddenly, my thoughts were interrupted by the clamoring of young voices telling me I was up and urging me to hit my serve. I was so discombobulated by the call that I swung through on my first serve and accidentally whacked my right kneecap. The pain was so intense; it felt as though I had broken my kneecap. After hopping around on one leg in excruciating pain and managing to hit a feeble second serve under the head shaking stare of my wife (who had absolutely no idea what I was doing), I returned to the task at hand—getting Sergio claimed by an NFL team.

When I got home that evening, I scoured and contacted my list of teams that either had interest in Sergio before the draft, interest in signing Sergio immediately after the draft, or had played against Sergio in the pre-season. Despite my efforts, Sergio was unclaimed and we decided to sign with New England on their practice squad. I continued to follow the waiver wire and team injury reports during the first few weeks of the regular season and contacted teams whenever an opportunity arose at safety (through waiver or injury).

Our break finally arrived during the fourth week of the NFL regular season. I received a text message from Eliot Wolf during halftime of the game between the Packers and Lions. Eliot was concerned that Green Bay had just lost their starting free safety, Morgan Burnett, a rookie third round pick from Georgia Tech, for the season due to a torn ACL. Eliot then asked if Sergio would be open to signing with the Packers to their 53 man roster if the spot opened up. Without hesitation, I said yes, so Eliot told me that Reggie McKenzie (then the Director of Player Personnel for the Packers and currently the General Manager for the Oakland Raiders) would contact me later that evening when the MRI results were made available. After informing Sergio of the news, I attended our weekly evening church service and went out to dinner with my wife at our favorite Italian restaurant in the East Village.

While at dinner, I received the call from Reggie. I spent the next 20 minutes on the phone with him, discussing the personnel situation in Green Bay, the possible opportunity and Sergio's interest in making the move. While Reggie couldn't make any promises, he did say he would let me know either way the next day. As I pondered the situation that evening and with no guarantee of the Packers actually making a move, I made up my mind to strike while the iron was hot. More specifically, my goal was to leverage the Packers interest to compel the Patriots to call Sergio up to their 53 man roster (where he would earn almost 4 times as much as his practice squad salary). I called Nick Caserio, Director of Player Personnel for the New England Patriots, on Monday morning and alerted him of the situation. The Patriots had traveled to Miami to play the Dolphins on Monday night, but Nick assured me that he would call me back upon his return to Foxboro on Tuesday morning. True to his word, Nick called the following day. As he explained, the Patriots just did not have a spot for Sergio on their 53 man roster, however, in a show of good faith and to convince us to stay rather than depart for another team, Nick offered to increase Sergio's practice squad salary to $250,000—which nearly tripled his previous p-squad salary of $88,400—to remain with New England.

We decided to take the deal, which was a smart move in hindsight because Green Bay ended up staying put and my client was now earning a paycheck nearly three times the size. Sergio remained on the Patriots practice squad for the next two weeks before I received a call on a Wednesday morning. The time had finally come and the Patriots wanted to sign Sergio to their 53 man roster before the Chargers game that Sunday. When it was all said and done, Sergio had received a signing bonus (which is unheard of for a practice squad player being called up to a team's 53 man roster) in the amount of $38,835, which was the exact same signing bonus the Patriots had given their last seventh round pick that year, QB Zac Robinson from Arizona State. Sergio's total signing bonus that year of $51,335 would've placed him 21st out of 48 seventh round picks as an undrafted free agent! Sergio made his NFL debut that Sunday on national television and ended up making the game-saving tackle on Chargers All-Pro tight end Antonio Gates. For his efforts, Sergio was awarded the game ball by Coach Bill Belichick.

As happy as I was for Sergio's storybook ending, I recognized another opportunity to strike while the iron was hot. The following morning, I sent the link to an online article in the Providence Journal (titled "In his NFL Debut, Sergio

Brown Saves the Game") to the Nike rep for the Patriots, George Balanis. I knew that George's son was an assistant coach on the Notre Dame men's basketball team and that he always had an affinity for Notre Dame players. My intuition was correct—we were able to parlay Sergio's game-saving efforts in his NFL debut into a three-year Nike deal!

Sergio's journey to the NFL exemplified excellence and perseverance to the highest degree. I have an undying obligation to pursue excellence for my clients at every level—whether they're an undrafted free agent or a first round pick. No matter what the odds, I have a binding duty to impart my absolute very best to every endeavor which I undertake on their behalf—knowing that in my hands I have been entrusted with their sacred, fragile dream. When your client trusts in you, commits himself fully to following your guidance and reaches the pinnacle of his lifelong dream, you find in the fleeting flash of victory, the super-charged fuel to continue to persevere no matter how bleak the circumstances, to move forward with confidence, vision and purpose… and to never say die.

Chapter 9

....

The Dotted Line

"Character may be manifested in the great moments, but it is made in the small ones."

~ Phillips Brooks

Looking back, it is amazing to see how one of the greatest opportunities of my life all began with a simple phone call. Life is an intricate series of divine appointments interconnected through space and time—and I was about to embark on a fascinating ride.

I had just gotten back to NYC from an ultra-productive weekend in Chicago where I had met with Robert Hughes (draft-eligible running back from Notre Dame) and my client Sergio Brown after the Patriots-Bears game in blizzard-like conditions on Sunday night. Upon my return to the office, I had several voicemails waiting for me and, as I hastily skipped through the messages, I came upon one that was a little different from the rest. "Hello, this message is for Eugene Lee. My name is Matthew Galkin and I am a producer working on an ESPN documentary on sports agents. Please return my call at…" I did a double take and hit the replay button immediately. I listened very intently this time around. To my surprise, the caller sounded legit and there was no doubt he referenced the most powerful four letter acronym in sports.

To say I was intrigued is an understatement. As hard as I was working to build my agency, the exposure from a well-produced ESPN feature would only serve to accelerate the continued growth of my athlete representation practice. On the flip side, I was certain that there would be major time and travel commitments involved along with fear of the unknown—allowing people "in" to experience the behind-the-scenes, inner-workings of my agency and my own personal life. After giving it some thought, I decided the good outweighed the bad. It was worth a shot.

I called Matthew back, he emailed me the project treatment and we scheduled an interview at my office the very next day. Matthew Galkin was an executive producer for Warrior Poets, a NYC-based production company owned by Academy Award nominated director and acclaimed filmmaker Morgan Spurlock. Warrior Poets were hired by ESPN to produce a one hour feature on the most ruthless industry in sports—athlete representation. Matthew looked the part of the New York documentary filmmaker/Brooklynite. Sort of indiscernibly young…heavy glasses…beard…and scruffy enough that no one who walked into the room would have trouble picking out the lawyer.

When I met with Matthew, I learned right away that he had already spoken to nearly a hundred agents, including some well-known heavy hitters, regarding involvement in this project. For a second, I caught myself in a moment of self-doubt. Out of that many agents, what made me different? Why would ESPN want to feature me instead of some of the higher profile, more established agents to whom Matthew had alluded? Was this merely an informational interview for the film? Although I looked Matthew squarely in the eyes, insecurity had my mind racing all over the place...until I looked within. I remembered the long drives, cold, rainy games, season-ending injuries, unexpected client waivers, fast food dinners at 1:00am and excruciating pain of being kicked in the gut from having come in second on a recruit. All that I had done and experienced up to that point in my career had led me to this God-given opportunity. And I was going to make the most of it.

I braced myself, took a deep breath and allowed the words to flow from my heart. I spoke with passion, enthusiasm and vulnerability as I discussed where I had come from, what I was doing and where I wanted to go. I talked about the challenge of building a successful agency without compromising your principles in such a cutthroat industry. I discussed my faith and how it played such an integral role in helping me to persevere in spite of the inevitable setbacks and disappointments associated with representing professional football players. Matthew was scribbling furiously on his notepad and we spoke for nearly an hour.

"What's the timeframe of the project?" I asked, as he was leaving.

"We'd like to begin shooting sooner than later, most likely before the end of the year," Matthew explained. I shook Matthew's hand and he told me he would be in touch. I had had enough great meetings that went nowhere in my career to know better than to get dreamy about the ESPN doc. Still, I left the office that evening with an eerie sense of peace. I had a strange feeling that, beyond the big-name agents, Matthew and his production team were searching for the right story to tell in this project. Against all odds, I had a hunch it might be mine. I expressed the same to my wife over dinner that evening. "I know it's crazy, but I just have this feeling that I'm going to end up being chosen for this project."

It was business as usual the very next day. With college bowl season approaching fast, I was in the process of scheduling final recruit meetings when I received an email from Matthew in the late afternoon. My intuition was correct. "We want to know what final recruit meetings you have lined up over the next few weeks and we want to start shooting this weekend," the email read. I nearly jumped through the roof of my office as I began fist pumping like Tiger Woods in his prime! I was absolutely thrilled and humbled for the life-changing opportunity (and a little nervous about what the future would hold), but there was no turning back now. I called my wife, let her know the good news and emailed Matthew back. The first stop on "The Dotted Line" world tour would take place that Friday in a small town thirty miles outside of Washington, DC called Manassas, VA.

Manassas was the hometown of my top recruit that year, West Virginia cornerback Brandon Hogan. After making arrangements with Matthew regarding the film crew meeting location, I double checked the address for Osborn High School where I was scheduled to meet with Brandon, his guardian Jeff Davis and his high school coach Steve Schultze on Friday afternoon. I beat the alarm clock as I jumped out of bed early the next morning, full of excitement for the first day of shooting and my final meeting with Brandon, the long-awaited culmination of several months of zoned-in focus and hard work. It was going to be an unforgettable day! My Delta shuttle flight to DC was only 40 minutes wheels up to wheels down, but I didn't need a plane to get down there that day. I was flying on a gamut of emotions.

I made my rendezvous with the Warrior Poets film crew at a hotel parking lot about ten miles outside of DC Matthew and his team had rented a regular sedan and a minivan to carry all of their A/V equipment. It was obvious from the sheer number of HD video cameras, boom mics, wireless mics, tripods and light reflectors that this wasn't their first rodeo. I was dealing with professionals in every sense of the word. The first order of business was for me to sign a release form and get mic'd up. This marked the first and only time in my legal career that I merely glanced over an agreement rather than devoting the proper time and attention to review it in detail, but I was so juiced up for the opportunity, I decided the minimal risk of libel was worth it. As the sound technician ran the wire through my shirt, Matthew gave me the shoot details. He would ride with me in the front passenger seat of my car and interview me for the next ten miles until we arrived at Brandon's high school. The production assistant and associate producer would follow in the sedan in order to shoot footage of my car driving to the meeting location. Now, up to that point in my professional career, I had given a few speeches at law schools and made an occasional television appearance or two, but I had never before been followed by a five-person film crew with all eyes on me. I could feel the butterflies start to churn in my stomach, but I took a deep breath, said a quick prayer and started the ignition.

Fortunately, I was able to overcome my initial apprehension and settled into a nice groove. Matthew asked a wide variety of questions about the upcoming meeting, the people who would be in attendance, what I liked most about Brandon Hogan, the logistics of Combine training, the breakeven point on pre-draft expenditures and what made my brand of representation different from other agents in the NFL player representation industry. Time flew by and other than quick stops at Subway (for a late lunch) and a Marathon gas station (for my pre-game ritual Sugar-Free Red Bull—as captured in the film), we arrived at Osborn Park High School fifteen minutes ahead of schedule. As I pulled in to the school parking lot and parked the car, Matthew advised me to wait in the car until the cameraman and boom mic operator were ready. Apparently, they wanted to film me getting out of the car and making my grand entrance to the high school where I would meet with Brandon. We were rolling live as I sauntered through the parking lot to the front entrance of the school, trying my best to act naturally and completely forget about the film crew that was in tow. As I went to open the door, I discovered very quickly that the door was locked. Without missing a beat, I tried the adjacent door. It too was locked. Trying my best to remain calm, cool and collected, I took a shot at door number three. To my dismay, it did not budge! Realizing now that all of this was on film, my heart started racing and I started praying for one of the final two doors to open. None of them did. My worst nightmare—that of being portrayed as a bumbling, inept agent—was coming true. Still, I tried my best to defuse the situation with a nonchalant epiphany of sorts. "You know what? Since we're meeting in the football office, that entrance is probably toward the rear of the school. That's where I should've gone. I'll head over there now," I reasoned. Matthew and the film crew couldn't have been more gracious as they nodded their heads in total agreement and followed me to the back of the school.

We were rolling live again as I approached the school's rear entrance. I confidently grabbed the first door and pulled.

To my horror, it did not budge! I frantically attempted door number two, three, and four. They were all locked! I began sweating bullets and my heart was beating out of my chest when my cell phone rang. I breathed a sigh of relief—it was Brandon's coach, Steve Schultze. "Are you guys close?" he asked. "Yes, we're actually at the rear entrance of the school by the football office, but all the doors are locked," I exclaimed. I made sure I said it loud enough so the film crew could hear. "No problem. I'll be right down," Coach Schultze replied. As soon as I got off the phone, I turned to the film crew. "That was Brandon's coach. He'll be right down to let us in," I reassured them. There were muted looks of amusement on their faces, undoubtedly caused by my inauspicious film debut. Still, I found solace in the fact that we would soon be in the school where I could meet with Brandon, throw down my final presentation with passion and precision and secure my first player commitment of the year.

A couple more minutes passed when my cell phone rang again. It was Coach Schultze. "Hey, I'm down here by the rear doors. I don't see you guys," he reported. "We're outside the doors. I don't see you either," I replied. It was at that moment that the light bulb went off. "Wait a second. Are you guys at Osborn Park High School? We're Osborn High School a half mile away," he explained. My jaw dropped and the revelation hit me like a ton of bricks. What were the odds in a small town in Virginia to have two high schools—one Osborn Park, the other Osborn—separated by half a mile? I could only shake my head in disbelief. Feeling like the Webster definition of tail between my legs, I broke the news to Matthew and the film crew. "Guys, I am so sorry, but I took down the address for the wrong high school. This is Osborn Park. Apparently, Osborn is half a mile away," I confessed. Matthew and the film crew were good-hearted about the mix-up and said it was no problem. I added some levity to the situation by asking Matthew not to use the footage of me being locked out of every door into the high school as the intro to the documentary with the bumbling cartoon melody ("du dunt, du dunt, du dunt") being dubbed in the background with Morgan Spurlock's voiceover as icing on the cake, "Meet Eugene Lee..."

Thankfully, the rest of the shoot went smoothly without incident. I was a little unsure of how I would present to a player with a film crew hanging on my every word, but when I got in the zone, I completely forgot that they were even there...and I delivered the presentation of my life.

Occasionally, I get a sense for how fortunate I am to be able to do what I do. Athlete representation is one of those industries where one day you can be on the field, watching a client play in front of 90,000 screaming fans on national television, and the next day, be in a high school football coach's office—surrounded by chalk boards, discarded equipment, and the stern faces of coaches tasked with vetting agents and protecting one of their own. Yet, I passed the test with flying colors.

"On a scale of 1-10, you were an 11," said Brandon's guardian Jeff Davis. "You hit a major home run here today, Eugene." When I departed Osborn High School that evening for Blacksburg, VA (where I would meet with Virginia Tech TE Andre Smith on Saturday morning), I had no doubt that Brandon Hogan was going to sign with me and that Matthew and his crew would capture our journey for the documentary. Coincidentally, I had the same feeling about the address for Osborn Park High School.

When I received the call from Coach Schultze the

following Monday informing me that Brandon would not be signing with me after all, I was completely flabbergasted.. Between failure and success, failure is the more tangible emotion. You stare out the window for a while. You re-evaluate decisions you made along the way, and wonder where it went wrong. You momentarily consider a different line of work. You call your wife. You wonder how this will play on an ESPN documentary.

But as you often do in this industry, I dusted myself off, got back on my horse and zoned in on my remaining recruits. Over the next couple weeks, I ended up signing Notre Dame running back Robert Hughes and University of South Florida linebacker Jacquian Williams. Matthew, Morgan and the rest of the Warrior Poets production team decided to follow my journey with these two players from divergent backgrounds. Robert was a heralded, big-time recruit coming out of high school from inner-city Chicago. He was a US Army All-American and signed with a prestigious program (Notre Dame) where he earned meaningful minutes as a true freshman. Jacquian was an unheralded recruit coming out of high school who attended Fort Scott Junior College before transferring to the University of South Florida before his junior year. With only one start during his junior season, Jacquian entered his senior season with no National or BLESTO grade. The plan was to show my entire pre-draft journey with each player from start to finish so the first step was to film the actual signing of their NFLPA Standard Representation Agreements ("SRAs"). Since Matthew and his crew already had footage of Jacquian signing his SRA after our initial meeting in Miami before the Orange Bowl (where I had flown down to meet with Virginia Tech TE Andre Smith), our next stop was Chicago, IL to film my signing of Robert

Hughes.

While at the Orange Bowl, I had received a last minute phone call from UConn linebacker Greg Lloyd, Jr. His father was a vicious, hard-hitting linebacker for the 1990s-era Steelers under Bill Cowher. Despite losing his starting spot early in the season to sophomore linebacker Sio Moore (future second round pick of the Oakland Raiders), Greg still received a Combine invite and wanted to set up final agent meetings in Nashville later that week. On a whim, I decided to fly to Nashville for a Friday afternoon meeting with Greg, then depart for Chicago early that Saturday morning to meet up with "The Dotted Line" film crew for my meeting with Robert. My meeting on Friday went well and I was in surprisingly good spirits—excited to sign Robert and film again in the Windy City—for my 6:00am flight from Nashville to Detroit on Saturday morning.

I landed on a frigid, but sunny morning in Detroit Metropolitan Airport around 8:30am EST and had about an hour and a half before my connecting flight to Chicago. I decided to grab some breakfast, but before sitting down, I thought about the day of filming that lied ahead and the natural rapport and friendship that I had so easily struck with Robert. I became more and more excited about my involvement in this project and what was to come over the next few months.

As I finished my breakfast, I began to think about filming at post-season all-star games, the Combine and the NFL Draft. Instinctively, I reached down to grab my iPad out of my messenger bag to confirm the actual dates. To my surprise, my messenger bag was nowhere to be found. I looked under the table, on the chairs, behind me and even around me. The bag had totally disappeared. Trying my best to stay calm, I retraced my steps back to the flight. And then it hit me. I had inadvertently left my messenger bag in the family restroom! I jumped out of my seat and sprinted toward it. My heart was racing when I arrived and turned the handle to the door. Although it had been nearly fifteen minutes since I had used the facilities, my hope was that no one had used the restroom in the interim or that someone had used it and left the bag to its rightful owner.

When I opened the door and surveyed the bathroom, my heart sank. My messenger bag was gone. My hope had turned into a pipe dream. As I began to take mental inventory of what was in the bag, my despair only deepened. The bag was a small treasure chest of Esquire magazine goodies—GPS, black dress watch, iPad, my favorite pair of Persol sunglasses (which I purchased on my honeymoon in Italy)—and, most importantly, it contained the SRAs. Despair gave way to a glimmer of hope as I visualized a scenario where a concerned citizen took the bag to a nearby restaurant or store. After quickly settling up my bill, I ran to a Japanese restaurant across the concourse. I described the bag in detail to the manager, but to no avail. I tried three more restaurants, a candy store and a newsstand, but the results were the same. Any shred of hope I had was fading fast and the hollow feeling in my stomach was growing by the minute. My last gasp attempt was the Westin Hotel in the McNamara Terminal. I was told by the newsstand manager that the airport hotel entrance had a lost and found and a police officer on duty. I ran to the hotel entrance, but should've taken a leisurely stroll. No dice, no bag. As I discussed filing a police report with the officer on duty, it suddenly occurred to me that I still had a connecting flight to catch! I had been so consumed with finding my bag that I totally lost track of time. I glanced down at my watch and it read 9:50am. Not a good sign if your flight is scheduled to depart out of another terminal at 10:10am. Leaving my bag behind left me with a tortured knot in my stomach, but I had a plane to catch. I took off in a full sprint down the escalators and through the underground walkway that connected McNamara Terminal with North Terminal. After five minutes of non-stop sprinting, I arrived at my gate for the final boarding call. Sweat was dripping off my face as I hurriedly boarded the plane—a small victory that helped ease the pain of my stolen bag. As I settled into my seat, I realized that during my mad dash to make the flight, my favorite Hugo Boss scarf had flown off my neck. It was a fitting end to a disastrous connection in the Motor City.

Despite the inauspicious start, our filming that weekend went relatively smoothly. At times, I couldn't help thinking about the logistical nightmare that awaited me upon my return to NYC—filing a police report and compiling receipts and credit card statements for my insurance claim—but as soon as my mind would begin to wander, the thrill and excitement of signing a top recruit in front of an ESPN film crew brought me back to the here and now and the amazing opportunity that lied ahead. Since my "real" SRAs were stolen with my bag, we had to improvise and print off a "fake" SRA from the NFLPA site for the signing in Robert's living room. Although the emotions were real and captured for posterity in the documentary, the actual signing occurred via Fed Ex the following week.

The next four months were filled with triumphs and disappointments for both Robert and Jacquian. From Combine snubs to official pre-draft visits, we experienced the peaks and valleys that were a precursor of what was to come in their future NFL careers. Robert ended up going the undrafted free agent route, signing with his hometown Chicago Bears after the lockout, while Jacquian ended up being drafted in the sixth round by the New York Giants. It was a major accomplishment for an under the radar player and was the glorious result of our plan to highlight his speed, athleticism and relative-value to linebacker-needy teams picking in the mid-late rounds of the draft. Getting the call from the New York Giants was one of the watershed moments in my career, because the agency had rolled the dice on a "fringe" prospect and, I feel, helped to strategically increase his value. Both parties were thrilled. Jacquian celebrated and cried with his family, and my team had a celebration of our own in the "war room" of our New York offices. The work, it seemed, was paying off.

The euphoria of the draft wore off quickly, however, and a little over one month after the draft, for reasons that only Jacquian can know, he terminated our agency relationship. It was the year of the NFL lockout so I thought financial distress may have had something to do with it. We also heard through the grapevine that Jacquian had received some bad advice from a former NFL player in Tampa who was pushing him to sign with his agent. I was reminded that it's impossible to be everywhere at once, keeping an eye on young clients all over the country, while less-scrupulous agents swoop in with promises of money.

With all that I had invested and the mountain we had scaled, I couldn't just throw in the towel. So I flew down to Tampa to meet with Jacquian face-to-face to get to the bottom of the situation. Our meeting went well and I confirmed that a major source of Jacquian's frustration was the lack of cash flow he was enduring due to the lockout. The lockout meant, practically, that we couldn't negotiate deals for our new draft picks, and players couldn't receive their signing bonuses. They were, essentially, in professional limbo. Although we had spoken numerous times since the draft, because I had not specifically asked him about his financial situation, Jacquian was under the mistaken impression that I just didn't care. I quickly refuted this point and vowed to be much more proactive in checking in on him and every aspect of his well-being going forward. I left our meeting with the reassurance that Jacquian would re-sign with me upon receipt of a new SRA. Alas, it was not meant to be.

Despite overnight mailing Jacquian a new SRA and pre-paid Fed Ex label upon my return to New York and following up with him diligently over the next couple weeks (and even finding him a part-time job at a local YMCA), I received an email from his new agent while driving back from Ohio in early July asking me to refrain from contacting his client. As upset and angered as I was, I vowed not to allow bitterness and vengeance to engulf my soul and detract from my ultimate purpose—which was to continue to grow my agency with integrity, creativity, vision and faith. Little did I know, I would soon be put to the test.

As the lockout ended later that month, I received an unexpected phone call from Matthew. "Hey Eugene, now that the lockout is over, we'd like to film you negotiating Jacquian's contract," he said. I hadn't spoken to Matthew since the conclusion of the NFL Draft nearly three months before so I was under the impression that our filming had concluded with Jacquian's selection in the draft. This was a total surprise and—in light of recent events—morphed into my worst nightmare real quick. After trying to think of ways to maneuver around the topic, I came to the stark realization that I was backed into a corner with nowhere else to go. I had to tell Matthew the truth. "Well, you're not going to believe this, Matthew, but six weeks after the draft, Jacquian ended up terminating my services," I revealed. "I did everything I could to salvage the relationship and even flew down to Florida to see him, but he ended up signing with someone else," I acknowledged. I could hear Matthew's jaw hit the ground on the other line.

"You have got to be kidding...that is unbelievable...I am so sorry, Eugene," he empathized. I was hoping that our conversation would end right there, but Matthew continued. "We'll want to get this on film. I knew it was a cutthroat business, but this is UNREAL," he said. My stomach dropped. After having been portrayed as an up and coming agent and protagonist over 4 months of filming, I now would have to own up to the fact that my marquee client terminated me a little over one month after THE biggest day of his life; after all of our hard work and sacrifice had culminated into the fulfillment of his lifelong dream. I could only imagine what viewers would think. What horrible thing could Eugene have done to deserve this fate? How competent of an agent could he really be to allow something like this to occur? In a cruel ironic twist, the biggest opportunity of my professional life was about to become the largest, self-imploding disaster of my career. As much as I wished I could've declined the interview, I had made a commitment to see this project through to the very end and fulfill my obligations regardless of circumstances outside of my control. So, that is what I set out to do. Matthew and I coordinated an interview date and time at my office early the following week and I trudged home, downtrodden and defeated, feeling like a man being led to the electric chair.

I spent every waking second that weekend preparing for

my interview. My biggest fear was that I would come across as weak in light of the unexpected termination. I did not want viewers to feel that I had been taken advantage of by a client who utilized my resources, scouting contacts and experience to rise to the pinnacle and then drop me like a bad habit for what he perceived as a better situation. I spent hours practicing my answers to anticipated questions in front of a mirror so I could not only gauge what I was saying, but the manner in which I was delivering the message. My goal was to come from a position of strength. I wanted viewers to understand that the termination did not tarnish our shining body of work in placing this young man in a position to achieve his dream. I wanted them to believe that it was truly his loss and that my agency would learn from this experience and move forward to bigger and better things.

Although I had my strategy in place, the more I practiced, the more anger and anxiety I felt. I still didn't understand why this was happening to me. How could I be given such a tremendous opportunity only to have it flushed down the toilet? It was at that moment that I understood the true meaning of humility—there is a God and I am not Him. The opportunity to be featured in this wonderful project was not of my own doing. It was a blessing from God. Although I didn't understand why it was me, out of hundreds of agents, who was chosen for this role, I accepted this divine appointment and moved forward in faith, secure in the knowledge that God was looking out for me; that He had a plan for my best. And just as I had trusted before, I would trust again. I would give the best interview of my life and allow God's will to take its course. Once I surrendered, I found an indescribable peace, a peace that accompanied me to my ESPN interview that week. Although it was the hardest interview of my life with Matthew asking pointed questions about my relationship with Jacquian and any professional shortcomings that could've led to the termination, I was able to impart dignity and strength and I have God's grace to thank for that.

One day after the Jacquian interview, Matthew and his crew shot footage of me negotiating Robert's undrafted rookie deal with the Chicago Bears. It would mark my final day of filming for "The Dotted Line." After we had agreed to terms and the crew began packing up for a celebratory lunch, Matthew came up with a brilliant idea for an ending sequence for the documentary. As I exited the building with my messenger bag over my shoulder, shades on and cell phone in hand, Matthew wanted to capture footage of me speaking on the phone with a recruit with the elevator doors slowly closing, thus creating an organic fade to black moment. The triumphant elevator exit would serve as a vivid contrast to the bumbling start to filming seven months before.

Although the plan was inspired, implementation proved to be a little problematic. In order to shoot the scene, I needed to be the only person in the elevator. Well, our timing was not the best, especially in a thirty story office building with nearly every employee headed out during the lunchtime hour. I must've called twenty different elevators before we finally found an empty one and stuck the ending. There was one sequence in particular when I walked toward a crowded elevator, did an about face, heard another elevator ping, walked to that elevator (which ultimately turned out to be crowded as well), did another about face, heard another elevator ping and walked toward elevator #3 (with the third time not being the charm). The crew and I were in tears, we were laughing so hard. To this day, I wonder what people in that office building must've been thinking when their elevator door opened, a man in sunglasses talking furiously on his cell phone approached quickly to enter, whirled around abruptly without missing a beat and exited stage left with film crew and boom mic in tow. It turns out the multiple takes were worth it in the end. The elevator sequence was used as the final clip in the ESPN documentary.

As the premiere approached, there was a sense of nervous anticipation because neither I nor any other agent featured in the documentary had seen any edited footage (including Josh Luchs who, even though we had never spoken or met during filming, unexpectedly, reached out to me a week before to congratulate me and wish me the best of luck in my future endeavors). Nervous, because what had, to that point, been a mostly private endeavor, with wins and losses endured in private, would now be made public. It made what we were trying to do more real and tangible and ratcheted up the pressure.

Yes, I would receive the occasional call from Matthew or Mike Rushton, an associate producer for Warrior Poets, with requests for statistical data, in which they would drop reassuring hints that editing was coming along well. However, I went into the documentary release completely blind; all I could do was rely on my faith. A couple weeks before the premiere, I received an excited phone call from a close friend of mine who had just seen me in a trailer on ESPN. The trailer sampled footage from AC/DC's "Money Talks" and when I watched it for the first time a couple days later, I had goosebumps as my adrenalin went into overdrive.

I rode a wave of adrenalin, excitement and hope all the way through the night of the premiere on October 11, 2011. As I gathered with family and friends to watch the documentary, a smile crept across my face, where it remained from the opening sequence of final recruit meetings (luckily, they did not include the Osborn Park High School footage) to the infamous elevator scene at the very end. The film depicted the divergent pre-draft journeys of Robert and Jacquian and my steadfast guidance and support as the one constant throughout. The documentary was a case study in filmmaking excellence and I could not have been any happier with the truthful portrayal I was given by Morgan Spurlock, Matthew Galkin and the rest of the Warrior Poets team. The outpouring of feedback from family, long-lost friends, professional colleagues, acquaintances and even total strangers was staggering and touched me to the very core of my being. Other than my wedding day, it was probably the most moving, humbling experience of my entire life.

I received emails from as far as the United Kingdom, Europe, Africa, Asia and Australia, all of which expressed support and admiration for how hard I worked for my clients, how much I cared and the upstanding manner in which I conducted my business. One email was from a father whose son watched the documentary and was now motivated to become the first person in his family to attend college to prepare for and pursue a career in the athlete representation industry. As the calls and emails continued to trickle in, I realized that my role in this documentary had fulfilled an even greater purpose. More than just a recruiting tool and my fifteen minutes, "The Dotted Line" allowed me to show viewers that you can excel, succeed and thrive in your calling without sacrificing your integrity or morals. If I could serve as that beacon of light for this cutthroat industry (oft-characterized by agent missteps that make the headlines) and motivate and inspire others to pursue their dreams by utilizing and maximizing the old-fashioned principles of hard work, creativity, perseverance and faith, then my involvement in this film would have been worth it even if I never signed another player.

It's one of the most contrived sections of dialogue in *Jerry Maguire*, but there is a grain of truth when Jerry explains that "we work in a cynical, cynical business." It's true. There are few "thank-yous" given or received. When I had agreed to participate in this project, I did so with the foolhardy belief that the filmmakers could only use what I would give them; that I could only be depicted for who I am and what I stood for. Subsequently, I learned the time-tested truth in Hollywood—that a gifted filmmaker can make you look any way he wants you to look. With that nuanced perspective, I owe a debt of gratitude to Morgan Spurlock, Matthew Galkin and the rest of the Warrior Poets team for their honor and integrity in making this film. Thank you from the bottom of my heart.

Chapter 10

....

Pay it Forward

"In the long run, men hit only what they aim at."
~ Henry David Thoreau

The first time I ever tried my hand at downhill skiing was during my junior year at GlenOak High School. Our Ski Club convened on a cold Saturday evening at Brandywine Ski Resort near Akron, OH. While it wasn't Vail, the slopes were still intimidating for someone who had never before donned a pair of skis. However, I reasoned that, as an athlete, I would be able to pick up the skill set without too much difficulty. So I did what most beginner skiers would do—I eschewed ski lessons on the bunny slopes and took the ski lift to the peak of the highest, steepest slope on the resort and learned on the fly as I flipped, fell and crashed my way down the slope. For some odd, sadistic reason, I kept count of how many times I had fallen on my way down the slope. By the time, I had reached the bottom, I had counted well over thirty times. It was a brutal experience, but I remained committed to learning how to ski in one night so I hopped right back on the ski lift to take me back to the peak where another brutal MMA session awaited. By the time the evening was over, I had accomplished my goal of learning how to ski, but as I slowly rolled out of bed the next morning, I began to realize the steep price I had paid for victory—aching joints, bone bruises and muscle strains over my entire body.

As illustrated by my self-taught skiing experience, when entering the athlete representation industry, there is often no better way to learn than through trial and error. However, going this route requires an unnatural willingness to accept the pain, hardships and turmoil you will inevitably experience along the way. To shorten the learning curve for those prospective agents who envision a future career in athlete representation and help you to avoid the same mistakes that I once made, I have compiled some practical pointers and insights that I have learned (often times the hard way) since breaking into this industry nearly eighteen years ago.

Scouting

Although quantified to a certain extent by forty times and measurements, scouting is an inexact science and, just like in baseball where the benchmark for a top hitter is a .300 average, player evaluation is an exercise characterized by more strikes than hits. My dear friend Jerry Angelo was a bastion of knowledge in terms of scouting and evaluating players and he was kind enough to impart some of his snippets of scouting wisdom to me. When scouting a player, simply take out your notepad and write down everything you see on the field—how a player changes direction, how he reacts in space, how adept he is at keeping his feet, how natural he is at catching the ball with his hands, how easy or difficult it is for him to get off blocks. By transcribing your visual evidence, you'll be able to go back, review your notes and start piecing together the scouting puzzle. NFL teams will always grade to a player's ceiling meaning they will evaluate a player's game film, determine the highest level of play he exhibits on tape and extrapolate to that sustained high level of play once the player gets to the next level. NFL teams are always looking for players with special traits—whether they are athletic, intellectual (i.e., football IQ), instinctual or intangible (i.e., toughness, competitive desire, leadership)—and, as the logic goes, agents should seek to sign these types of players too. In projecting HWS (height/weight/speed) ratios and athleticism to the next level, always keep in mind that the farther away you get from the center of the field, the more gifted the player needs to be athletically, which makes perfect sense when you compare the raw athleticism, speed and explosiveness of interior linemen with cornerbacks and wide receivers. Although defensive backs are typically the most gifted athletes on a team, instincts in coverage are what separates cornerbacks from safeties in the defensive backfield.

I am a firm believer that in addition to a player's physical and athletic traits, it is imperative to represent young men of character. Players who know the difference between right and wrong and make decisions on and off the field consistent with their faith-based principles. Character by itself will not raise a player's draft grade, however, the lack of character (as manifested through failed drug tests, arrests, academic ineligibility, suspensions and feedback from coaches) will drop a player's draft grade faster than a feather tied to an anvil. There are several NFL teams that will red flag a player and take him off their draft board completely due to questionable character and significant off-the-field issues. Moreover, when there are two or three players on a team's draft board that are graded equally, NFL teams will look to character as the differentiating factor, or the tie-breaker. Representing young men of integrity also promotes and enhances productivity within your organization. Because there are no fires to put out, no clients to bail out of jail in the early morning hours and no emergency press conferences held in crisis management mode, you can devote your time to more productive pursuits including recruiting prospective clients, pitching clients for endorsement and sponsorship deals and marketing draft-eligible and free agent clients to the right NFL teams.

When it's all said and done, scouting is still an inexact science and sometimes there are no plausible explanations or logical reasons for how circumstances pan out. Despite thousands of hours of intensive film review and millions of dollars spent on scouting, occasionally a player does slip through the cracks of NFL teams.

A couple years ago I represented a linebacker from Auburn named Daren Bates. Daren was an undersized, playmaking linebacker who led his team in tackles with over 100 tackles in each of his junior and senior seasons despite playing weakside linebacker in the SEC at 215 lbs. Since Daren started at strong safety during his freshman year before converting to linebacker, we marketed him as a projected safety at the next level during the pre-draft period. Daren was not a Combine invitee, but had a very good workout at the Auburn Pro Day. However, Daren was not selected in that year's NFL Draft and, despite our dogged efforts (and calls made to all 32 NFL teams), the only offer we had from an NFL team was an invitation from the St. Louis Rams to attend rookie minicamp on a tryout basis. This was not entirely a surprise. Les Snead, the General Manager for the St. Louis Rams, was a former Auburn tight end who always had a soft spot in his heart for Auburn players. Year in and year out, you could count on at least 2-3 undrafted Auburn players to dot the training camp roster of the St. Louis Rams.

However, we were still one step shy of our goal. All we had on the table was a pre-paid flight to attend and participate in rookie minicamp with no guarantee of an actual contract. I reluctantly made the call to Daren and explained the situation. We were both flabbergasted that after a four-year career as a starter in the SEC, this was the best and only offer we had on the table. However, we both agreed that we had no other choice. As soon as I hung up the phone with Daren, I received a phone call from Ran Carthon, Director of Pro Personnel for the Rams. "Eugene, we actually want to sign Daren to a contract," he explained. I did a double take and confirmed what I had just heard. "Just so I'm clear, no tryout anymore? You want to sign him to an actual contract now?" I asked. Ran confirmed. As this was our only offer, I had no leverage for a true negotiation, but the opportunity was the real payoff. We agreed to a three-year deal with no signing bonus. With the odds stacked against him, as one of 22 undrafted free agents signed by the Rams that spring, Daren ended up making the Rams final 53 man roster that fall and the following season. He is now entering his third season in the NFL as living testament that you can never overlook the size of a player's heart—the one measurable that cannot be readily quantified.

Recruiting

When I first started in the industry, I mistook quantity of travel over quality. I felt that I had to be on the road every single weekend or else another agent would swoop in to commandeer the relationships I was painstakingly building with my recruits. To that end, I spent thousands of dollars on recruiting trips that were comprised solely of a handshake, hello and five-minute face time after a game with players who were not overly responsive to my pitch or whom I ultimately did not end up signing.

Over time (and I credit getting married and my newfound awareness of time spent away from my wife and family for my enlightened perspective), I learned to travel and recruit smarter. Yes, it is imperative in this industry and critical for success to hit the road and build relationships with players and their families nationwide, but you should have a strategic plan in place and confirmed meetings set up beforehand so you can maximize the value of the trip and the associated travel expenditures. I'm a big fan of "two for one" trips where I will fly to a home game at a school located in an NFL city, attend the college game and meet with my recruit on Saturday and then attend the NFL game on Sunday to see my client. Through trial and error, I've discovered that it is much better, both fiscally and emotionally, to cut your losses early in recruiting. If a young man is fixated on signing with IMG or another huge corporate conglomerate (and all of the advantages and disadvantages that come with the territory), then I am not going to change his mind and sell him on my agency no matter how hard I try. It is simply impossible to fit a square peg into a round hole. I would rather make more efficient use of my time and resources in recruiting players who want to be a part of what we are building, what we stand for and what we have to offer.

Once you have identified players whom you believe would be the right fit, the next step is to know the gatekeeper. "Knowing the gatekeeper" means to recognize which parent or family member will hold the key to the information gathering process. You can have the most dynamic presentation prepared, but if you do not disseminate this information to the right person within a player's inner circle, it will fall on deaf ears.

I learned this lesson the hard way in my recruitment of former Vanderbilt and current Green Bay Packer cornerback Casey Hayward. When I began recruiting Casey during the summer before his senior year, he asked me to funnel information through his family so he could concentrate on the season. I respected his wishes and began speaking with Casey's father. I followed up diligently after our initial conversation, sent him materials on my agency and continued to pass along NFL scout feedback during the course of the season. Over the next few months, we began to develop a nice camaraderie and I was under the impression that the family (and Casey) would delve in to the agent selection process and final meetings toward the end of the season. I couldn't have been more wrong.

At the Vanderbilt vs. Florida game that fall (which I attended to see Casey and Jeff Demps), I made a quick introduction to Casey and his father after the game. As I was about to leave, Casey's mother came over and made a quick introduction. We exchanged pleasantries, I gave her my business card and continued on my way. I didn't think anything of it until I received a call from Casey's mother later that evening. "Hello Mr. Lee? This is Tish Hayward. I wanted to thank you for coming to the game today and for the interest you've shown in Casey. Unfortunately, we've been narrowing things down and have our final group of three agencies selected," she explained, "You seem like you run a first-class operation. I wish we could've spoken earlier in the process."

My jaw hit the floor. I tried to convince Ms. Hayward into reconsidering my agency by telling her I had been communicating for months with Mr. Hayward, but her mind was already made up and it was too little too late. I was on the outside looking in because I had mistakenly assumed that Casey's father was the gatekeeper.

Although I had a difficult time deciphering the gatekeeper in the Hayward family, I had no such problem during my recruitment of former Stillman College and current Tennessee Titans nose tackle Sammie Lee Hill. I met with Sammie's parents on a crisp, sunny Saturday morning at a KFC located in a gas station just off Interstate 20 outside of Tuscaloosa. I had flown into Birmingham earlier that morning and was driving northeast on I-20 to meet with the Hills before attending the LSU vs. Auburn game later that night. I arrived a few minutes early and took a seat at a table by the corner window. No sooner had I sat down, an oversized Ford F-150 pulled up to the gas station. The doors opened and Sammie's mother got out on the driver's side while his father exited on the passenger side. She was a relatively short woman, but she navigated the considerable distance between the cab and ground by stepping down first on the running board before descending to the pavement. Sammie's father was a large man—at least 6'5" and a lean 220 lbs.—however, when the meeting began, there was no question who was the gatekeeper in that family. After I gave my presentation and answered some questions, the Hills departed with Sammie's mother climbing back in to drive the massive pickup truck with his father sitting meekly on the passenger side. Make no mistake about it, Sammie's mother was definitely driving the truck in that family—both literally and figuratively speaking.

One of the most difficult skills to learn in recruiting is the ability to say no. Given the significant upfront cost involved in training players for the draft, you must be very careful about making the investment only in players whom you believe are going to make NFL rosters and earn commissions for your agency. The hard part involves breaking the news to a player whom you have recruited and developed a relationship that you won't be able to sign him and pay for his training. A few years ago, I recruited a running back from Auburn named Onterio McCalebb. Onterio was blazing fast, but during the course of a subpar senior season (both for Onterio and the team), NFL scouting concerns such as lack of size, lateral quickness and vision began to manifest themselves.

Upon the conclusion of the season, Onterio reached out to me, eager to sign and begin training for the draft. However, based upon my own evaluation and feedback from NFL teams, I had come to the conclusion that Onterio was, at best, a priority free agent. Given his status as a fringe prospect, there was way too much risk involved in incurring thousands of dollars in upfront training costs—costs that might never be recouped. Nevertheless, I had an obligation to treat this young man's dream with dignity and respect by being completely upfront with him. I called Onterio back and told him that the only way we could sign him was if he would agree to train at school. I explained my reasoning which included a real-time assessment of his draft grade and a detailed explanation of the back end cost recoupment structure for NFL agents. As expected, Onterio did not end up signing with me, however, I hoped he could only respect my honest opinion and respectful delivery. To be fair to Onterio, he ran one of the fastest 40 yard dashes in the history of the NFL Combine at 4.28, and, although undrafted, is still in the league as a cornerback with the Cincinnati Bengals.

In recruiting, you'll often be asked by players and their parents whether you plan on signing and representing multiple players at the same position in the same draft class. There is no right or wrong answer to this question. With no guarantees of a player commitment until an SRA is actually signed, agents are required to play the percentages and recruit multiple players, often at the same position. If by chance, an agent is fortunate enough to sign more than one player at a particular position, the argument then becomes that NFL teams will grade and evaluate players based on their own scouting. All that an agent can do is provide the most favorable, up-to-date information on a player in order to compel teams to grade that player at his ceiling.

An agent has no control over a team's internal player evaluation protocol, so as long as he is providing the same type of information for all of his clients (even those who play the same position) to NFL teams in a timely manner, then he has done his job with absolutely no conflict of interest. A related school of thought centers on the projected draft grades of the players in question. If you are representing two cornerbacks, but one has a first round grade while the other has a late round grade, the conflict is not necessarily there because there would be such a huge disparity between the players on a team's draft board (i.e., there is no chance the late round player would be drafted over the first round player). Now, in a scenario where you are recruiting only one player at a particular position, you could easily take the opposite stance. You could then argue in good faith that it is impossible to allocate your time and efforts equally between two players. At the end of the day, an NFL team can only select one player at a particular position in a particular round so regardless of your efforts at magnanimity, one of your clients will inevitably end up with the short end of the stick. Whether you sign multiple players at the same position or only one, the key is to play to your strength.

Over the last few years, as the number of underclassmen declaring for the NFL Draft has risen dramatically, I find myself being asked more and more for guidance by underclass players and their parents as they face one of the most important decisions their family will ever make. With career-ending injuries a stark reality of the game and no guarantee of increased productivity the following year, the "strike while the iron is hot" mentality manifests itself every year toward the end of college football season. When faced with the question of whether or not a player should declare for the draft, I like to tell recruits and parents the following. If you are a first round lock, then you should absolutely declare. If you are a second round lock, then you should probably declare. If you are a third round lock, then you should maybe declare after taking into account all extenuating circumstances. However, if you receive a fourth round grade or lower, then you should stay in school. For me, advising a player to make the right decision to stay in school is nearly as gratifying as signing a top round pick because you are safeguarding and investing in his future, both in the short and long-term, both on and off the field.

Post-Season All-Star Games

As more post-season all-star games have begun to dot the NFL pre-draft landscape, the decision of whether or not to play has taken on much greater significance. In addition to long-time standbys such as the Senior Bowl and Shrine Game, fledgling games such as the NFLPA Collegiate Bowl, Medal of

Honor Bowl and College Gridiron Showcase have offered an even greater number of draft-eligible players a prized platform to showcase their skills to NFL teams. While receiving an invitation to an all-star game is a tremendous honor, it may or may not be conducive to furthering a player's NFL prospects.

When determining the overall value to your client of playing in an all-star game or not, an agent must always remember that there are three possible outcomes of participating in an all-star game…and two are bad. Your client could simply have a bad week of practice and hurt his draft stock. Or, your client could get hurt which would limit his training or altogether prevent him from participating in his pre-draft workouts at the Combine or his pro day. The best case scenario is that your client has a stellar week of practice and improves his draft stock, but even then, the ultimate effect on his draft grade must be tempered by the level of competition at the game. That is why it is imperative to examine the roster of your client's team before committing to play in an all-star game.

A premium is placed on practices at post-season all-star games so it behooves an agent to make sure that the level of competition on the opposite side of the ball on his client's own team is good enough to justify the risk of playing in the game. For instance, if you are representing a cornerback, you want to make sure the receivers on your client's team are good enough to legitimize a strong week of all-star game practices. The same analysis holds true for other positions, including defensive ends and offensive tackles, outside linebackers and tight ends and defensive tackles and interior offensive linemen. Now, if you are a Division II player who receives an invite to an all-star game, then it makes sense to participate because you'll be playing up to a higher level of competition than was shown on tape from your senior season. Conversely, if you are a highly productive multi-year starter for a big-time program from the SEC, Big Ten, ACC, Pac 12 and Big 12 (the "Big 5"), other than the Senior Bowl and possibly the Shrine Game, participating in any of the newer all-star games is a decision that must be painstakingly evaluated with the level of competition scrutinized with a fine-toothed comb, because you will likely be playing to an equal or even inferior level of competition from the competition you faced all season long. If tape from your senior season against Big 5 conference competition jumps off the screen, then the risk of playing in a newer all-star game outweighs any possible benefit that could be gained.

Although tickets are sold for the game, all-star game practices are the real event; where players can make real money by improving their draft stock. In fact, after player arrivals on Sunday and weigh-ins on Monday, you can rest assured that every NFL scout, coach, personnel director and GM in attendance will be watching intently from the stands for every team practice from Monday through Wednesday of all-star week. By the time the actual game rolls around on Saturday, almost all NFL personnel will have already left town to head home and prep for the next all-star game on the agenda. That does not mean that NFL teams do not care about the game though. Contrary to popular belief in the agent community, not only do NFL teams receive footage of the actual game, they will watch and evaluate game performance. Therefore, an agent should prepare his client and emphasize the importance of finishing the week out strong. In terms of an unofficial ranking of all-star games, I have always advised clients to play in the Senior Bowl (unless you are a lock #1 or #2 overall pick or an underclassman in which case you would not be able to participate anyway) and consider playing in the Shrine Game (unless you produced All-American caliber tape from a Big 5 conference and need additional training time to address athleticism concerns at the Combine). The decision to play or not to play in any of the other all-star games will come down to your client's level of competition on tape (i.e., is your client from a smaller program who will be playing up to a higher level of competition?), the level of competition on the opposite side of the ball on your client's own roster and the importance of stellar workouts and testing numbers for your client during the pre-draft evaluation period.

The Senior Bowl in Mobile, Alabama is the ultimate football experience. Attended by the best college players and nearly every NFL scout, coach, and decision-maker in the business, it is a veritable feeding frenzy. The lobby of the Senior Bowl hotel is packed with NFL team gear and apparel. You might run into a GM or head coach at one of the dive bars surrounding the hotel. Everybody is angling for an opportunity at the Senior Bowl. Even the guy modeling gear at the Under Armour booth used to be somebody…used to play in the league. Even HE is looking to get back into the game. It's exhilarating and nerve-wracking all at the same time. You feel like there's a finite amount of time to make the most of your connections.

But the real joy is the football—watching the best players in the country do what they do. Where else can you watch Hall of Fame linebacker Mike Singletary run defensive drills, and then watch that year's crop of blue-chip quarterbacks trying to see who can throw a ball through one of the gates in the upper reaches of Ladd-Peebles Stadium? All under the attentive eye of NFL legends past and present. Just being there is a privilege.

The Combine

National Football Scouting ("NFS") is the organization that runs the Combine. During the Combine selection process, a six-member selection committee will vote on each draft-eligible player on their master list. If a player receives a unanimous six "yes" votes, then he receives a Combine invite. If a player receives five "yes" votes, then he goes on the "bubble" list. If a player receives four or fewer "yes" votes, then he does not receive a Combine invite. The initial round of Combine invitations go out in late December/early January and are emailed to players who have either completed their seasons or finished playing in their bowl games. About 65 Combine invitations are withheld from the initial round to account for underclassmen who declare for the draft in mid-January. Once the early entry list has been finalized, it is then received and reviewed by NFS and a second round of Combine invitations goes out toward the end of January. This second round is comprised of underclassmen and seniors on the "bubble" list who receive the requisite six "yes" votes when the selection committee reconvenes and votes again.

When I first started in the business, I made the mistake of thinking more is more when it came to Combine training. I thought that the more time my client had to train, the faster he would run, the higher he would jump and the more reps he would bench at his pre-draft workout. I learned the flawed logic behind that way of thinking very quickly. One of my first non-Notre Dame clients was a defensive end from Duke named Phillip Alexander. Duke ended their season early with no bowl game invite so Phillip began training during the week of Thanksgiving. Phillip trained intensively for nearly 14 consecutive weeks before participating in his pro day workout at Duke that March. Despite over 3 full months of training, Phillip didn't test or perform anywhere near what he was capable. His legs felt dead as he labored through the workout and his heavy breathing caused him to bend over in exhaustion several times during his positional drills. In his defense, Phillip came down with a nasty chest cold a couple days before his pro day, but I believe that too was the result of a compromised immune system from a body worn-down and beaten up from excessive training. Once you get beyond a certain training threshold (typically 8 weeks), the law of diminishing marginal returns inevitably kicks in. In fact, as was the case with Phillip, too much training can actually undermine and even detract from optimal athletic performance. With all the training in the world, you are not going to take a 4.7 player and turn him into a 4.4 player. The human genetic code simply cannot be manipulated in that manner.

The purpose of Combine training is to teach and familiarize players with the various Combine tests including the pro agility and 3 cone, tweak and refine running technique and starts (which may help shave a tenth off a forty time), coach players on position-specific drills and train players—in the weight room and on the treadmill—to show up for the biggest job interview of their lives fit, in shape and in excellent cardiovascular condition.

As illustrated by the proliferation of Combine training facilities over the past decade, players and agents have become all too obsessed with the almighty Combine invite. However, getting invited to Indy does not guarantee anything except for an opportunity to work out for, and interview with, NFL teams in one convenient location. Contrary to popular belief, a Combine invite is not an indicator of a player's draft worthiness or future NFL success. The numbers do not lie. There are approximately 325 players invited to the Combine. Approximately 40 non-Combine invitees are drafted every year. Since there are 255 total picks in the NFL Draft, this means that 215 Combine invitees are drafted by NFL teams. Well, if only 215 Combine invitees get drafted, what happens to the remaining 110 invitees? The answer is that they either go the undrafted free agent route or are waiting at home for the phone to ring. The harsh reality of the Combine is that 1 out of every 3 players in Indy will not be drafted by an NFL team.

After the Combine, every NFL team is allotted up to thirty official pre-draft visits. Pre-draft visits are typically reserved for first-round players for whom a team wants to perform additional due diligence (due to the value of the pick), players with off-the-field character or health issues that a team wants to fully vet and players who were not invited to the Combine, but had stellar pro day workouts. The importance of the pre-draft visit to the latter group cannot be underestimated. Since an NFL team will not draft a player without a full medical on file, pro day workout warriors are flown in primarily to be evaluated by a team's medical personnel. I've had clients in the past wonder why, despite being a Combine invitee and one of the top players at their position, they received only one pre-draft visit. The answer is straightforward. If your client is a kid with no off-the-field issues who tested well at the Combine, checked out clean medically and received glowing reviews from his school's coaching staff, an NFL team is going to save its pre-draft visit for another player for whom more due diligence needs to be performed.

At the end of the day, the Combine is a whirlwind experience jam packed with impromptu NFL meetings, media dinners and client counseling. It is a place where unlikely dreams are made and tenuous hopes are dashed. Over the past few years, the Combine has grown in popularity and scale to become a media event to rival the NFL Draft and Super Bowl. Yet despite the ever-present laser-sharp focus ingrained in NFL personnel, agents and players, there is an underlying sense of fun and a "go with the flow" mentality that pervades the festivities.

You can always expect the unexpected in Indy. Every year, the second floor of the Omni is transformed into a carnival-like atmosphere with booths and suites for a wide array of vendors vying for the attention (and endorsements) of these future professionals. You'll have footwear and apparel companies such as Nike, Under Armour and Adidas, sport supplement companies such as Muscle Pharm and even custom clothiers such as Astor & Black staking their claims to valuable parcels of real estate on the Omni mezzanine. Players and agents can be seen with goodie bags of samples and free gear as they hop from station to station checking out the wares of these modern-day, gridiron traders. Several years ago, it just so happened that the Indiana Home Schooling Association had scheduled their annual convention during the same weekend as the NFL Scouting Combine. The hallways of the Indiana Convention Center were teeming with NFL personnel hustling to attend on-field workouts and player interviews all the while juking and dodging Mennonite and Amish women scrambling to attend their next workshop. It was a fantastic spectacle of the most unlikely juxtaposition. As I navigated the hallways, all I could do was take in my surroundings, smile and thank God for being part of the show.

Media

Like Jim Carrey's character from "The Cable Guy," the media can either be your best friend or your worst enemy. As an agent who fully understands and appreciates the power of the pen, I have always preferred the former. I have thus made it a priority to cultivate strong relationships and friendships with NFL media nationwide. The relationship between the media and an NFL agent is one of a symbiotic nature. It's akin to a "you scratch my back, I'll scratch yours" dynamic. If a reporter is looking for the scoop on a possible free agent signing or team interest in a high-profile draft eligible player, he will call the agent. Similarly, if an agent is looking for some positive press for a client or insider feedback during training camp practices or away games, he will contact and leverage his media contact(s).

A few years ago, I was on the road driving back from a recruiting trip on a Sunday afternoon. My client, Sergio Brown, had just broken into the starting lineup for the New England Patriots who were playing the Buffalo Bills on the road. Without satellite radio, I had no way of catching the game myself, however, I did know someone who had a bird's eye view, my friend and ESPN Boston reporter Mike Reiss. I had always given Mike non-privileged information about Patriots clients and over the years, we had developed a solid friendship. I drew upon our foundation of goodwill when I texted Mike to ask him how Sergio was playing. Mike texted me right back with a detailed description of a couple big plays and even one pass interference penalty (hey, I had to respect the journalistic integrity). Right then and there, I understood the fundamental principle of Media 101—if you go above and beyond in your dealings with the media by offering them accurate and timely information on your clients, they will do the same for you when you need it most.

Over the years, I have been blessed to have built friendships with well-respected reporters and writers from a variety of media outlets and publications nationwide including ESPN, NFL Network, ESPN New York, ESPN Boston, ESPN Chicago, ESPN Dallas, USA Today, Detroit Free Press, Chicago Sun-Times, Atlanta Journal Constitution, Comcast SportsNet and the New York Daily News. The NFL media is a tight-knit fraternity that will welcome you in to their inner circle only after you have earned the trust of one of their brothers. Such was the case when my good friend and former ESPN New York reporter Ohm Youngmisuk introduced me to his good friend (and now mine) Ebenezer Samuel, Giants writer for the New York Daily News, a few years ago.

A bunch of us including Ohm, Ebenezer, Sean Jensen of The Pioneer Press and Dave Birkett of the Detroit Free Press had gotten together for dinner at the Combine at an Italian restaurant in downtown Indy called Lorenzo's. It was the first time I had ever met Ebenezer and after a few requisite questions about clients at the Combine and pending free agency, our discussion turned to training. Ebenezer was a self-confessed gym rat who loved hitting the weights. I had always been a workout fiend myself so we struck a common ground as our conversation ventured into Hans and Franz territory for the remainder of the meal. A few days later, I received a call from Ohm. "Yo, you threw Eb for a loop! He has always been obsessed with getting strong and jacked in the gym so his diet has been pretty much Muscle Milk and supplements, but you sat there at dinner eating pasta and meatballs, really enjoying your food … and you're still in good shape!! You threw him for a loop, man. He's wondering if he's doing something wrong," Ohm recounted.

I couldn't help but laugh at Ohm's version of events. A couple weeks later, Ohm forwarded me a text from Eb. The text said, "I'm hitting it hard now. I'm eating more, getting leaner, getting stronger. I think Eugene has a bigger frame than me." I did a double take. He said what?!? I was rolling in laughter. It was at this point that I decided to have a little fun. For the next couple months, I would draft concocted texts about Eastern European workout routines and training methods and send them to Ohm, who would in turn forward them to Eb. My favorite one incorporated the following, "Ohm, I read in a Russian medical journal (formerly Uzbekistan) that to stimulate muscle growth when you workout, you should hold your breath during hard cardio. Whether you are running sprints or lifting heavy weight, you should hold your breath the entire time."

Ohm forwarded that text to Eb and sent me his epic response. Eb wrote that he researched it online and could not find anything scientific to validate this theory "although a modified Valsalva Maneuver might be comparable." Eb's reference to the Valsalva Maneuver (which involves a forceful attempted exhalation against a closed airway, i.e., a closed mouth) startled me because I started to believe that Eb might just give it a shot. For his safety (and to assuage concerns over my own legal liability), I had to let the cat out of the bag. As I offered my mea culpa, Eb could only laugh as he welcomed me to the brotherhood. We have helped each other out on numerous occasions over the past few years, from me providing him with access to clients to him offering me information from closed training camp practices. Our friendship illustrates the symbiotic dynamic between an agent and a member of the media at its finest.

Climb the Mountain

Every agent who enters the industry does so with dreams of representing the next Rod Tidwell. The most exciting and intriguing aspect of representing professional football players is that your fortunes can change instantly with the signing of one player, one first-rounder, future All-Pro with Hall of Fame caliber ability. Yet the allure of instant gratification can also provide a foothold for greed which can ultimately tempt you into overlooking your moral code, sacrificing your principles and, ultimately, taking slippery shortcuts to success.

I was confronted with this dilemma when I first entered the industry over fifteen years ago. It was late August and I had just finished my second year of practicing law in NYC while representing a few Notre Dame players on the side. I was contacted by a man (let's call him James) and his cohort (let's call him Rich), who had picked my name out of the NFLPA contract advisor directory. James and Rich were based out of Greenwood, Mississippi and came to me with an enticing proposition. They were allegedly the advisors for star Ole Miss running back Deuce McAllister, widely regarded as the top running back in college football and one of the top players in the 2001 NFL Draft. Now, I hadn't launched my own agency yet, but I was starting to lean in that direction, so the appeal of signing and representing arguably the #1 pick in the NFL Draft was not lost on me. I heard them out.

"Yeah, Lee, you know, we've been looking to partner up with a younger agent, the right agent, to represent Deuce in the draft and make sure his needs are met during the season.

We found your name in the directory and after doing some research, think that you are our guy," James explained. He continued, "We'd like to set up a meeting sooner than later so we can introduce ourselves to you and get everything in motion for the upcoming season." I was utterly dismayed and dumbstruck at my good luck. Having grown up in Canton, I had learned the art of being street smart so I began to pepper James and Rich with questions about Deuce. What was his real name? ("Dulymus.") What was his hometown? ("Ludlow.") What was his National grade? ("7.6") Their answer to my final question surprised me and led me to believe that these guys were legit because they had access to the very same National Football Scouting reports used by NFL teams (and lucky agents) in the pre-draft evaluation/recruiting period.

Buoyed by their knowledge of Deuce and apparent legitimacy, I booked a flight to Jackson, MS the following week. I met with James and Rich for a quick dinner at a local seafood restaurant in Greenwood. James was thicker set with scars on his forehead from an apparent halo brace while Rich was wiry in build with fidgety mannerisms, but both seemed focused on the task at hand, which was getting Deuce on board with the right agent so he could stay focused on football during his senior season. I spent a couple more days with James and Rich in Greenwood, even attending a Mississippi Valley State game against Delta State, and when it came time for me to leave, we agreed on a handshake that I would be Deuce's agent once the season was over. As I flew back to New York, I couldn't help but think of my astronomical luck; that this was too good to be true. And, unfortunately, it was. No sooner had I returned to NYC than I received a phone call from James.

"Hey, Lee, I was fittin' to head up to Oxford to visit Deuce this weekend and need some money for gas, hotel and food. Can you wire me a few hundred dollars? I can send you my account information," James asked. I was still excited about the prospect of representing arguably the best player in the draft so I didn't think too much of the request. I wired James the money for his trip. A couple days later, I received a call from Rich. He too wanted to hit the recruiting road, but his trip had nothing to do with Deuce. He wanted to visit a linebacker from North Carolina named Sedrick Hodge that he would "obviously send my way" and needed money for a rental car, gas and lodging. I reluctantly wired Rich the money he requested, but from that point on, my guard was up.

It all finally came to a head a couple weeks later. I received a phone call from James (with Rich on the line) telling me that Deuce was short on funds and needed money ASAP. James asked me to wire the money to his account and he would in turn drive up to Oxford to hand the money to Deuce in person. My stomach dropped. What James was asking me to do went against every ethical and moral fiber in my DNA. Moreover, I didn't fully trust James at this point. For all I knew, any money wired to his checking account would never leave the account to see the light of day. But, the devil on my other shoulder was playing the advocate—what if James and Rich were telling me the truth and Deuce really did need the money? I had a once-in-a-lifetime opportunity to represent possibly the #1 pick in the entire draft. The temptation was overwhelming. I decided to gather some more information. "James, I have never had even one conversation with Deuce. How do I know you guys really know him and are telling me the truth?" I asked. I continued, "I'm not doing anything until I know that you guys really do know him." James offered a short retort, said he would be in touch and angrily hung up the phone. I breathed a sigh of relief figuring the decision had already been made for me ... until I received a phone call from James a few days later.

James was calling me from a jewelry store in Oxford and he was not alone. He was apparently looking at watches with Deuce. James put Deuce on the phone. "Mr. Lee, this is Deuce. James told me that you're the one looking out for me," he said. I remained unconvinced. "Deuce, if this is you, what's your real name?" I asked. "It's Dulymus. Man, why you ask me that?!? You don't think this is really Deuce?" he steamed. "I need money, man, and James said you were my guy," he said. Feeling like I was in an episode of The Twilight Zone, I asked Deuce to hand the phone back to James. "James, I'll be in touch in a couple days," I said. I hung up the phone and placed my head in my hands. At this point, I wasn't even sure which way was up or down. There was a very strong likelihood that James had hired one of his homeboys to pose as Deuce as part of his ongoing scam to extort money from me. However, there was also the miniscule, snowflake's chance possibility that I had just spoken to Deuce and could cement his commitment to me as his agent by sending him the money. I was torn.

I knew the right answer, but the temptation was overpowering. Right then and there, I understood that this was going to be a defining, watershed moment in my professional career and in my personal life. I couldn't afford to make the wrong decision, but I didn't know where to turn. So I turned to God and received the guidance I was seeking. I looked within and was reminded of how I was raised by two loving parents and the values that were instilled in me, the example I wanted to set for my younger brother, the inner peace and self-respect I sought and fought for every day of my life by doing the right thing in the midst of evil and chaos. A little voice in my head reminded me to, "Never put passion before principle because even if you win, you lose." My decision was made. I called James and Rich back later that day and terminated all dealings with them. In hindsight, neither James nor Rich had any affiliation or association with the real Deuce McAllister. They had hired an impostor to pose as Deuce in the jewelry store and were using the ruse as a way to extort money for themselves. It was a sad attempt to ensnare a young agent with the lavish spoils of representing a first round pick, but fortunately for me, I had some "help" in making the right decision. I never heard from James or Rich again. My only hope is that they found enlightenment and mercy in God's perfect time.

From this moment on, I would never take the slippery slope to success, but would climb the mountain one step at a time with secure handholds and footholds along the way. It would take time, but I would eventually get to the top and the view of the sunset would be utterly breathtaking for I will have earned every last bit of it through my toil, sacrifice and unshakable faith.

Chapter 11

....

Timshel

"Sometimes in life, you just have to tackle Yoda."
~ Eugene T. Lee

To succeed in the NFL player representation industry, you must have singular focus and tunnel vision. The smell of pigskin should be embedded in your DNA. You must eat, breathe and live football. My life is God, Family, Football, 24/7/365. However, apart from the extraordinary dedication and steadfast commitment required, I believe it is imperative to have the wisdom, courage and open-mindedness to seek out, savor and apply lessons learned from a wide assortment of real-life experiences to your work for your clients as an NFL agent. This is a grandiose way of saying that we should all learn from our mistakes.

I have always lived life relentless with an open mind to take advantage of opportunities as they arise to broaden the depth of my experience; to add vibrant color to the spectrum of my existence. I've been blessed to experience a full gamut of life-changing events that have helped shape and define me as an agent and as a man. Yes, I have made mistakes on the road to enlightenment, but the well-rounded perspective on life I have gained and the joie de vivre I have cultivated and nourished have been worth any growing pains endured along the way. Which is another grandiose way of saying that walking in my shoes is fun, and, at times, a real trip.

One of the most unique experiences of my entire life occurred when I happened to cross paths with a Broadway legend over fourteen years ago. I was still practicing law, but was on the verge of launching my own agency. My brother and his girlfriend were traveling back to Ohio from Boston and made a pit stop to see me in New York. I made reservations for us at Tao and we were seated on the second floor in full view of the giant two story Buddha.

We had just finished our appetizers when a woman from the large round table next to us approached our table. "Excuse me, but are you a personal trainer? I ask because we're with Tommy Tune. Tommy just got back to New York from Vegas after wrapping EFX and needs a personal trainer," she asked. I was completely caught off-guard, but never one to shy away from a challenge (or an adventure), I decided to answer her truthfully, but with a hint of chutzpah. "I'm actually a lawyer, but I'm an athlete and know how to train," I replied.

Intrigued, she continued, "Would you be interested in training Tommy?" Realizing this was turning very quickly into a crazy story to one day tell the grandkids (or put into a book), I confidently countered, "I'm not a certified personal trainer, but I've been training for years and know my stuff. I could definitely train Tommy. Here is my card." I had convinced her. "Great! I'm the sister of Tommy's assistant Peter so we'll be in touch tomorrow to set up an interview between you and Tommy. Thanks so much!" she exclaimed.

After she had left, I looked over at my brother and his

girlfriend. They were staring at me with eyes wide open, unsure and unbelieving of what had just transpired. I was still trying to figure out how she was able to peg me for a trainer so I did a quick inventory of my outfit. I was wearing a t-shirt and corduroys, but the shirt was rather snug. Ah, that was the personal trainer calling card! The next step was to perform some reconnaissance and find out more about Tommy Tune. The name sounded familiar and he was obviously some type of celebrity, but it wasn't until I got home that evening that I was able to piece it altogether via the Internet. Tommy Tune was a nine-time Tony Award winning performer, dancer, choreographer and director. He was a Broadway icon who at 6'6" was one of the tallest performers to ever take the Broadway stage. This guy was definitely a big deal.

Still, when I arrived at my office the next morning, the chance meeting from the previous night had all but slipped my mind. I did not expect it to amount to anything more than a crazy New York moment, a story to recount to friends over drinks at our next gathering. And then my phone rang. "Hello, Eugene. This is Peter, Tommy Tune's assistant. Tommy would like to meet with you this afternoon to discuss his training. Are you available at 3:00p.m.?" he asked. I couldn't believe this was happening! They had called my bluff and now it was time to put up or shut up. "Yes, I'll be there," I replied.

Tommy lived in a majestic high-rise condo on East 89th Street between Madison and Park Avenue. As soon as I walked in the lobby, I couldn't help but overhear the doorman giving instructions to a grocery deliveryman. "Mr. Brooks is expecting the delivery now. Please head on up," he directed. Mel Brooks lived in the same building. I could only shake my head. Tommy lived in a duplex penthouse with a beautifully landscaped, wraparound terrace that ran the entire length of the apartment. After a quick introduction, Tommy and I sat down in the living room where we got down to business. He asked me about my training background and proposed training regimen while discussing his fitness goals. "I want to build strength and muscle mass while keeping my flexibility," he explained.

As we neared the end of our conversation, Tommy pulled out a Chanel notepad where he wrote down his phone numbers and the name and phone number for his personal trainer in Vegas. I had never before seen a Chanel notepad, but I was more captivated by Tommy's signature. It was the coolest, most distinctive John Hancock I had ever seen. The letters of his name were written over a musical scale with a note hanging to the right of "Tune". Given my lack of a professional certification or real-world experience as a personal trainer, I decided it was probably a good idea to protect myself and draft a waiver for Tommy to sign prior to our first training session. The waiver would essentially discharge and release me from any and all liabilities, claims, damages or injuries incurred or sustained by Tommy during our training sessions. I showed up for our first day of training with the waiver in hand. Tommy signed the waiver and we headed to the weight room downstairs.

After the first couple sessions, it became clear that the same qualities that had made Tommy such an accomplished performer translated to his work in the weight room. He was a hard worker who pushed himself to complete every rep I had prescribed in every set.

However, I had a more difficult time. I was waking up at 5:30am every morning to get my own workout in before cabbing to the Upper East Side, training Tommy, cabbing back home to shower and get dressed before heading to the office by 10:00am. It was a grueling schedule and after our second full week of training. I did not know how much longer I could continue this exhausting pace. As divine intervention would have it, the answer was not one day longer. I received a phone call from Tommy's assistant Peter early the following week. Tommy had apparently pinched a nerve in his neck and was in extreme pain. He needed to cancel our training sessions indefinitely.

As Peter was explaining the situation, Tommy grabbed the phone. "Okay, I'm hurt. I'm hurt bad. Now, you gotta figure out what you did to make me feel like this. You made me do those military presses behind the neck," Tommy interjected. I bristled at the accusation. Having endured years of rotator cuff and shoulder issues, I had always made it a point to perform only front military presses. I would never do behind the neck military presses myself, let alone include them in a training regimen for Tommy Tune. "Tommy, I've had shoulder problems myself. I can assure you that I never had you do behind the neck military presses," I responded. "Oh, yes you did," he countered. "Oh, no I didn't," I declared. Realizing this was quickly turning into a he-said, she-said scenario with no clear victor in sight, I apologized to Tommy for his injury, wished him a quick and speedy recovery and asked him to contact me when he was ready to begin training again. Alas, the call never came.

It was a bittersweet ending to an unbelievable chapter. There would be no more training sessions with Tommy Tune, but I had a remarkable story to tell for the rest of my life and, more important, I learned an invaluable lesson that would serve me well for the rest of my professional career. Having Tommy sign the injury waiver protected me from any potential liability resulting from his pinched nerve. The same long-term perspective of envisioning every possible worst case scenario for my client and drafting contractual language to protect his interests would become the defining characteristic of my negotiation strategy. It is the agent's job to think of everything that can possibly go wrong, and then use that information to protect his client at all times.

With the Tommy Tune training experience ingrained in my subconscious, you would've thought I would've remembered to think through the ramifications of my behavior at the first holy communion of a dear friend's daughter a few years later. The day started off normally as I dressed in my best suit and tie and hopped on a train out of Grand Central Station to make the 90 minute trek north to Danbury, CT. The church was bustling when I arrived with my college roommate Carlos and his family and as we made our way to our seats, Carlos introduced me to the priest who would be presiding over the ceremony. "If you need a cantor, just let me know, Father," I quipped. "Thank you so much, but we are all set," he assured me.

I didn't think anything more of my attempt at small talk until a few minutes before the ceremony, when the priest spotted me and hastily approached my pew. There was a sense of urgency in his stride so I had a feeling something was awry. My intuition was correct. "Excuse me, sir, but our cantor has not shown up. If you're still willing to sing, we could definitely use your help," he pleaded. My stomach dropped. There was no way this could be happening. Why did I have to be the funny guy? My feeble attempt at humor was coming back to bite me on the behind. Carlos, his wife and in-laws were all staring intently as I pondered my decision. It was put up or shut up time. "Sure. It would be my pleasure," I replied. Having no idea what I had gotten myself into, I made my way out of the pew, followed by the astonished looks on the faces of Carlos and his family.

The butterflies in my stomach were dancing up a storm as I followed the priest to the cantor lectern to the right of the altar. I felt like a death row inmate being led to the electric chair. We reviewed the order of songs from the hymnal before the priest dropped another bombshell on me. "Well, not only did our cantor not show, but our pianist didn't make it either. You don't mind singing a cappella, do you?" he asked. The situation was quickly going from bad to worse. "Not a problem at all," I confidently feigned.

I took my seat and a sense of dread washed over me. I could definitely sing, but karaoke was much different than leading the congregation at a first Holy Communion celebration, let alone one involving my dear friend's daughter. I had always tried to live my life with integrity which for me was simply being a man of my word; following through on my commitments and doing what I say I am going to do when I say I am going to do it. My character and resolve were being tested now and although the stakes did not seem as great as an NFL player contract negotiation, they were to me for I knew the decision I would make would define me for the rest of my life. I felt like a prize idiot for writing checks with my mouth that my vocal cords couldn't cash.

I had to come through. I said a quick prayer, asked God for strength and channeled Nike. I just did it. I led the congregation in the first hymn (and even raised my hand to encourage the congregation to sing as I had seen many cantors do before) and, surprisingly, my fear dissipated. Before the responsorial psalm, I noticed a well-dressed Indian man approaching the lectern from the far right aisle. "I can play the piano. If you give me the song list, I can accompany you," he whispered. Apparently, his wife had talked him into helping a brother out. "That would be awesome," I thankfully replied, as I went over the remaining hymns with him.

The rest of the service went smoothly, although we almost hit a snag during the communal hymn. The song was "One Bread, One Body" and due to the number of first communion recipients, I ran out of verses to sing. I sang through all three verses again and even a third time before my eyes darted to another set of verses that had not yet been touched. The verses were in Spanish and as I approached the end of the refrain, I was *this close* to taking the plunge. Thankfully, discretion got the better part of my limited Spanish vocabulary and I circled through the English verses for the fourth and final time. The ceremony ended without incident and numerous parishioners, including Carlos and his family, came over afterwards to thank me and my new friend for helping make the service a special one for their child. I breathed in a sense of relief and gratification, thankful for the role I was able to play and with a renewed commitment to live my word as my bond in the NFL player representation industry and beyond. At the same time, I was chastened and humbled by the experience. It was a very vivid reminder not to play fast and loose with my own limitations.

Humility can be learned not only through real-life experiences, but by living an open-handed life and putting the needs of others before your own. Pope John Paul II summed it up best when he said, "The human being can fulfill the self only through self-giving."

It was the selfless desire to offer my mom comfort and companionship after the unexpected passing of my father that led to an unlikely and unexpected addition to our family. Two months after my father's death, I decided to fly home to Ohio to celebrate Mother's Day with my mom. I was still practicing law at my firm at the time and my assistant brought up the idea of getting a kitten for my mom. Her rationale was that my mom would want companionship with my father gone and kittens/cats are low maintenance. Now, I had always been a dog guy growing up (Rottweilers and Boxers were my favorite breeds) and didn't particularly care for cats so I wasn't completely sold on the idea.

Nevertheless, this time it wasn't about me, it was about my mom, so on a sunny Saturday morning one week before I was scheduled to depart, I found myself at the International Kennel Club across the street from my apartment. I asked the salesperson if they had any kittens in stock. Without uttering a word, she asked me to follow her to the back of the store where she led me to a small cage filled with a dozen Gremlin-looking creatures crawling all over one another. She explained to me that they had just received a shipment of pure bred Burmese kittens from Okie Dokie Cattery in Oklahoma. And yes, that is a real name.

Intrigued by these funny looking creatures, I asked her to pull one out. The first kitten she pulled out had no fear at all. He was so precocious—he crawled up my arm and sat on the back of my neck. When I pulled him off and held him on his back, he did not squirm at all, he sat there on his back with total trust and peace in me. I was sold on the spot. I told the salesperson that I had to run to a haircut, but if I decided to come back and buy a Burmese kitten later that day, I wanted to purchase this one so I asked her to write down his collar number—which she did. I returned later that afternoon and bought the kitten. I named him Kyle and brought him home with me. After running around and acclimating himself to my apartment, Kyle came over to me while I was sitting on my futon watching TV and climbed up and sat on my lap as content as could be with his tail wagging furiously.

I flew home that Friday after hosting Kyle for one week and surprised my mother with her Mother's Day gift which I pulled out of an otherwise innocuous carry-on bag. My mother was surprised to say the least and she gave it her best go—raising an energetic, overly affectionate kitten with loads of personality—but after a year and a half when I flew home for Christmas, my mother re-gifted Kyle back to me. Her exact words were: "I raised two boys, I don't want to raise a third." The decision for me was a no-brainer. Kyle was family now and my responsibility.

So, we flew back to NYC together and Kyle became my bachelor companion and family for the next four years (at which point, he became "adopted" by my wife Leslie). I know the adage that a dog is man's best friend, but those dog owners never met my cat and those who have—even people deathly allergic to cats—all love and adore Kyle. Kyle is a dog trapped in a cat's body. So much so that his nickname is "Dog Cat." From greeting me at the front door every evening when I would come home from work to licking me and flopping at my feet to show his affection, Kyle is the definition of unconditional love.

Kyle is a very vocal cat with an oversized personality. I don't know of many cats who will answer when they hear their name—but that is Kyle. Back in my bachelor days, every night when I was ready to turn out the light and go to bed, I would whistle and no matter where he was located in my apartment, Kyle would come running, jump into bed and curl up in my arm like a football to go to sleep.

As an extension of our family, we often take Kyle on trips and that has led to some interesting episodes to say the least.

On one occasion, Leslie and I had flown down to Fort Myers (with Kyle, of course) to visit my mother before taking a short road trip across Alligator Alley for a business meeting in Homestead, FL. When we checked in at the Holiday Inn Express, we discovered that the hotel did not allow pets. So, we did what most loving pet owners would do when faced with the same dilemma. We snuck Kyle in. After settling in to our room, Leslie and I went out to grab dinner.

When we came back to the hotel after our meal, we were greeted by the night manager. "Excuse me, sir, but do you have a black cat in your room?" he asked. I decided to play dumb. "Why do you say that?" I replied incredulously. "Because a security guard was walking around the hotel grounds this afternoon and saw a black cat sitting in the window of your room," he explained. I looked him squarely in the eyes and responded with conviction, "No, we do not have a black cat." But I could not tell a lie. "He is actually sable," I confessed. "They'll probably hit you with a pet cleaning fee. I think it's around $250," he advised. Alarmed and frustrated by the fact the pet fee was more than the cost of our room, I took down the name of the hotel manager (Latonya) and made a mental note to discuss the situation with her when we checked out of the hotel.

Sure enough, when I received the bill the next morning, there was a $250 pet cleaning fee added to the incidentals. I tracked Latonya down and turned on every ounce of charm I had. I pleaded my case as to why the pet fee should be waived—how we didn't want to leave Kyle alone by himself at my mother's condo, how the room was left in mint condition with no damage because Kyle was a very clean, declawed, short-haired cat, how he was such a beloved member of our family. Luckily for me, Latonya was a kind, compassionate soul and agreed to waive the fee. Ecstatic, I handed her my business card. "Thank you so much, Latonya. If there is anything I can ever do for you, please do not hesitate to let me know," I pledged.

I didn't think anything more of the incident until a year and a half later when Latonya called me out of the blue. "Hello Mr. Lee, this is Latonya from the Holiday Inn Express in Homestead. You gave me your card last year and said I could contact you if I ever needed a favor. Well, I have a huge one to ask. The owners of this hotel are opening up a new Holiday Inn Express a few miles away and are throwing a grand opening party in a couple weeks. I wanted to see if you could make a couple calls and get Ray Lewis and Dwayne "The Rock" Johnson to the grand opening. We would love for them to attend," she stated matter-of-factly. There was a moment of awkward silence as I replayed what I had just heard. Did she really just ask me to reach out to Ray Lewis and The Rock? Yes, she was dead serious. As respectfully as I could, I explained to Latonya that while I would totally love to help her in any way that I could, making a couple calls to get Ray Lewis and Dwayne "The Rock" Johnson down to Homestead, FL for the grand opening in two weeks was a bit out of the realm of my own possibilities. I think she believed me when she hung up the phone, but to this day, a part of me feels that she thinks I was holding out on her by not utilizing my connections. Needless to say, I don't think we'll be taking Kyle with us on the next trip to Homestead.

Over the years, Kyle has given me an enlightened perspective on my irrevocable duty as an NFL agent. At times, the NFL player representation industry can be just as unpredictable as caring for a cat. I have a daily obligation to look out for Kyle, knowing full well that without the food, water and shelter I provide, he could not survive on his own. His very existence depends on my unwavering commitment, diligence and care. The same holds true for my NFL clients. Their livelihoods depend on my daily commitment and diligence to the task at hand; guiding and nurturing their NFL careers with varying doses of technical expertise, motivational support, creativity, industry connections and faith. There is a tremendous responsibility that comes with representing an NFL player and it is one I would never underestimate or take for granted—a fundamental principle ingrained in my soul by the unforgettable escapades of the world's most loving Burmese cat.

Although there has been a practical sensibility to the lessons I have gleaned from real-life experiences (such as raising a cat), there was one experience in particular that became the lesson in and of itself; a life-defining mantra that would go on to motivate, fortify and uphold me through the inevitable peaks and valleys of life as an NFL player agent. During my third year of law school, my brother David and his frat brother, Brian Hallisay, flew out to Notre Dame over Halloween weekend to catch the Navy game. Brian was a finance major who would go on to leave a career on Wall Street to become a rising young actor in Hollywood. It was Brian's first experience at a Notre Dame home football game so we had an entire weekend of fun-filled events planned.

The festivities kicked off with a Halloween costume party at Heartland Brewery hosted by the law school in conjunction with the business school. It was a typical law school party with clusters of students milling around the dance floor with mixed drinks in hand. After a while, in an effort to "lively up" the atmosphere (as Bob Marley would say), Brian and I made our way on to the dance floor and began throwing down our best dance moves. Brian was a natural dancer and as I tried to keep up with my best Napoleon Dynamite, I gazed around the room and realized that we were the only two people in the entire venue who were expressing themselves freely and thoroughly enjoying the moment. To me, dancing was a metaphor for life. It is the purest form of expression in which the mind, body and soul are interconnected and people reveal themselves for who they really are with no inhibitions whatsoever. As I walked off the floor, I began to contemplate the meaning of my own existence. And then it hit me. I could never lose the joie de vivre that had helped to define my soul. I would make it a priority to live life relentlessly, savoring and cherishing every single moment, blessing and opportunity. I would fully commit to living on the razor's edge of youthful indiscretions and passionate thirst for growth and fulfillment—in any career, any endeavor, and any relationship. I would strive for the courage to maximize my talents and gifts to cultivate and create a life uncommon.

Emboldened by my newfound epiphany, I looked around to see my classmates huddled in their cliques of conformity until my gaze settled on a startlingly authentic-looking Yoda standing by the bar. "Brian, how funny would it be if somebody ran over and tackled Yoda," I asked. It was an absolutely preposterous notion, one that required nerve, courage and a dose of controlled insanity, however, I had just recommitted to a life of non-conformity and there was no turning back now. Before Brian could even answer, I took off. I sprinted ten yards across the room and laid Yoda out with a picture perfect form tackle. Yoda's drink went flying up in the air as he landed on his back with me on top. No sooner had we hit the ground than my mind began processing the ensuing dialogue at ultra-sonic speed. I had to feign a case of mistaken identity. "Yeah, man!!! Wait, I'm so sorry! I thought you were someone else," I sheepishly confessed. Other than being completely startled and confused, Yoda was no worse for the wear and accepted my apology. I helped Yoda up, brushed him off, bought him another vodka tonic and headed back to my brother, Brian and Tomas. Their reaction was priceless. It was a mixture of gut-busting laughter combined with a slight hint of fear and incredulity at what they had just witnessed. Little did they know that what I had just done would become the watershed moment that would define my approach to life from that day forward.

Over the years, life has brought with it many other opportunities to "tackle Yoda"—the day I decided to leave the firm and start my own agency, the day I asked my wife to marry me and the day I had to get over the loss of a client on national television and get back on the proverbial horse. In those situations, we rely solely on courage and faith. At the party it was pure impulse and a desire to carpe diem and suck the marrow out of life, and the moment. In adulthood, it has become a more nuanced, responsible and thoughtful response—but every time I pick up a phone to cold-call a recruit, I am tackling Yoda. Every time I get on a plane to go see a player and his family, I am deciding to charge off the stool and make something happen.

Despite the best laid plans of mice and men, there will always come a time where you will need to throw caution to the wind and move forward confidently armed only with conviction of purpose, strength of character and faith in God. Seal said it best when he sang "we're never gonna survive unless we are a little crazy." Sometimes in life, you just have to tackle Yoda.

Epilogue

······································

"For I know the plans I have for you,' says the Lord. 'Plans to prosper you and not to harm you, to give you a future and a hope.'"

~ Jeremiah 29:11

Life is an endless labyrinth of doors, continually opening and closing while the earthly maze is navigated by the compass of faith. Since writing this book, I have seen the hand of the divine doorman continue His work in my life.

I have teamed up with veteran agent C. Lamont Smith and a group of young, highly qualified agents, all possessing the Warhol Effect, to launch my new NFL player representation agency called MBK Sports Management Group, LLC. With a nationwide recruiting platform, we look forward to positively impacting and guiding the lives of aspiring NFL players for years to come.

In addition to forming the new agency, I have taken an Of Counsel position with the Chambers-recognized Sports & Entertainment group of the law firm of Garvey Schubert Barer. With a client roster of high-profile athletes and entertainers, my association with the firm has allowed me to provide my NFL clientele with an extensive offering of legal services and support while allowing me to expand the scope of my legal practice to clients in the music and entertainment industries.

Beyond the professional realm, I have been blessed to cultivate meaningful, authentic friendships with highly respected icons from the sports and entertainment industries. From meeting my brother and acclaimed actor Omari Hardwick in the gym of our building to meeting the former president of CBS Sports and sports television pioneer Neal Pilson on the set of Bloomberg Surveillance, I have seen the almighty hand at work on a daily basis.

The road that lies ahead is one I will travel with an eternal purpose. I am committed to using the platform I have been given to continue to change lives for the better. I will continue to give back, pay it forward, inspire and influence the lives of young men; to help them achieve their dreams, provide for their families, give back to their communities and use their platform as an NFL player to make a difference in lives across the world. Then, and only then, will I have fulfilled my God-given purpose.

For, I am my brother's keeper.

Acknowledgments

....

I would like to thank the following people without whom this book would not have been written: David Lee, Ken Dunning, Jerry Angelo, Eliot Wolf, Tyreo Harrison, Lamont Bryant, Deveron Harper, Brian Witherspoon, Carlyle Holiday, Mike Richardson, Deon Anderson, Scott Pioli, Chris Hall, Dwayne Harper, Jeremiah Warren, Daren Bates, Tomas Longo, the late Charles Rice, Michael Moorer, Tommy Tune, Mickey Marotti, Andy Reid, Tom Heckert, Art Shell, Justin Tuck, Ryan Grant, Marcus Freeman, Eddie McGee, Reggie McKenzie, George Balanis, Matthew Galkin, Morgan Spurlock, Casey Hayward, Sammie Lee Hill, Onterio McCalebb, Phillip Alexander, Ohm Youngmisuk, Ebenezer Samuel, Brian Hallisay, Jacquian Williams, Sergio Brown, Robert Hughes, Brandon Hogan, Steve Schultze, Jeff Davis, Kyle Lee, Renee Fountain, Adam Slutsky, Ted Kluck and Omari Hardwick.

Last, but not least, to every client who entrusted me with their career and the laughter, tears and joy we shared during our NFL journey. Thank you for believing in me.

Websites and
....
Social Media

Websites

http://eugenetlee.com/
http://mbksports.com/

Social Media

Twitter: https://twitter.com/EugeneTLee
Instagram: https://instagram.com/eugenetlee/
Facebook: https://www.facebook.com/EugeneTLee